P9-CPY-090

PROCLAIMING
THE WORD

PROCLAIMING THE WORD

Ronald E. Sleeth

new york • Abingdon Press • nashville

PROCLAIMING THE WORD

Library of Congress Catalog Card Number: 64-10605

SET UP, PRINTED, AND BOUND BY THE PARTHENON PRESS, AT NASHVILLE, TENNESSEE, UNITED STATES OF AMERICA

Dedicated to the memory of
HALFORD E. LUCCOCK
a master teacher who encouraged
his students to be *disciples*
not of Luccock but of
his master, Jesus Christ

PREFACE

Proclaiming the Word takes seriously the task of preaching. It affirms that the preacher's role is a theological one; that he is fulfilling an indispensable aspect of God's revelation to man. In this sense, this book is as basically concerned with the *why* of preaching as it is with the *what* and *how*. Therefore, the pages that follow take seriously the theological revival of the past few years which is predicated on the Reformation doctrine of the Word.

Related to the theological basis of the office of preaching is the stress laid here on *biblical* sermons. This approach is part of the same revival, for the Reformers' obsession with the Word was based upon the unalterable assumption that this Word was found primarily in the Bible. Hence, the emphasis upon biblical preaching as the normal stance for the Protestant pulpit. Although there may be room for other types of pulpit discourse, this book stands unashamedly on the platform that Christian proclamation is biblical.

Although indebted to the theological-biblical renaissance, I have pursued two other aspects of preaching which differentiate this book from some works which purportedly are theological in their emphasis—especially among writers who are overly influenced by continental theology. First, there is an attempt to relate the Word to the people in the pew and to the culture they represent. This concern for communicating the gospel rests upon the theological assumption that revelation is situational. If the Incarnation is to have meaning, then it has meaning at the point of making it relevant to man in his setting. Hence, this book is vitally interested in the *communication* of the gospel.

Second, there is a corresponding emphasis upon the role of the preacher in the preaching process. This book affirms that God has chosen the preacher to be his spokesman, herald, ambassador. In this sense, the preacher is intricately involved with the Word itself. Although the Word is not to be thought of subjectively in the sense that it is the preacher's word, neither is it true that the Word is wholly objective apart from the preacher's personality. Phillips Brooks's definition of preaching as "bringing truth through personality" is still a good platform for the modern preacher. Indeed, this is one way of seeing how the Word is to be incarnated.

It is hoped that this book can serve as a basic introduction to preaching for the seminary student and fledgling minister. For the pastor it can be a refresher course in homiletics, and perhaps enlarge and deepen his concepts of the importance of the preaching task.

My indebtedness in these pages is immense—perhaps more to the unnamed than to the named. I think of teachers, fellow preachers, colleagues, members of pastors' schools, and a host of students who have all heard these theories expounded in one way or another. Portions of chapter 1 appeared in *Encounter,* Vol. 19, No. 2, Spring, 1958, pp. 123-30. The substance of chapter 7 appeared in *Southern Theater,* VII, 3 (June, 1963), as "Religion and Modern Drama." Specifically, I am indebted to three of my colleagues. Professors John C. Irwin and Leander Keck read portions of the manuscript, and James Sellers read the entire book. Many of their invaluable criticisms have been incorporated with real appreciation. None of these men, however, is responsible for any inadequacy of idea or infelicity of expression. A final word of thanks should go to Mrs. Jean McMahon, who handled the typing with diligence and dispatch.

RONALD E. SLEETH

CONTENTS

CHAPTER I

Proclaiming the Word Through Pulpit and Sacrament

In each age the pulpit needs to restate its purpose. At the present time, as in other periods, there are challenges to the preaching task. Everyone is familiar with the attacks from without the church as to the futility of the sermon. But even from within there are questionings as the church seeks to find the basic nature of its ministry. Recent studies of the ministry which seek to define the minister's role are examples of the searching questions being raised about preaching and the other traditional roles of the ministry. There is an earnest endeavor to find some unifying factor underlying the gospel which can describe, if not define, the nature of the ministry. To those who hold to the centrality of the preaching task, these challenges force a re-evaluation of the role of the preacher in present-day Protestantism.

To speak of the "role" of the preacher is to examine the basis for preaching. Much of the concern in homiletics has been for the *how,* with a recent concern for the *what.* But a discussion of the role examines the *why* of the preaching office. In fact, such an examination might be called "the theology of the office of preaching."

The Reformers emphasized the Word of God as a basis for authority. What is often forgotten is that, for the Reformation thinkers, this Word of God was, above all, a preached Word. At the same time that there has been criticism of the place of preaching in the church, there has also been a restatement of the importance of preaching. This re-emphasis of the importance of the preacher's role has come, not from defensive preachers, but from modern theologians who, in the recent recovery of biblical and theological studies, have sought to capture again the primacy of the Reformation doctrine of the Word. Without necessarily embracing the theological systems of these writers, it is imperative that the modern-day preachers and the church which seeks to define the role of its ministers come to terms with what the theologians are saying about the primacy of preaching.

It should be pointed out immediately that the recovery of the importance of preaching by the theologians is not necessarily a defense of present-day preaching practice. Actually, it may be more judgment than comfort. If one considers preaching merely as an adjunct to the ministry, or as a technique, or as religious oratory, or as a talk on some topical subject at the eleven o'clock hour on Sunday, then he can derive no comfort from these writings. In other words, effective speaking on a superficial level is not preaching the Word of God. The preacher is being called to task for not understanding what the Word is and for not understanding what his role is in proclaiming it.

A careful study of the plethora of books on theology and homiletics demonstrates this emphasis on the preaching of the Word. What is read might be stated succinctly: the Word of God (or the gospel) cannot be separated from its proclamation. That is, the gospel is a preached gospel. The content cannot be separated from its delivery. As H. H. Farmer, a preacher-theologian, states, "The means and the content, the preaching and the message, are indissolubly one and cannot be separated from one another." [1] He contends that witnessing to the event was indeed part of the event. Farmer goes on to say what to some may appear as too extreme a statement: "Whoso said Christianity, said preaching." [2] And Emil Brunner, speaking along the same lines, ties preaching to the existence of the church itself. "The basic or primal function of the Church is that of preaching, for it is this which establishes the Church in every sense of the Word." [3] But lest one would think these are all theologians of a like mind, listen to an Anglican speaking for a branch of the church which is often accused of depreciating preaching. "The Christian preacher is an instrument by which the Church, the body of Christ, fulfills its function as the extension of the Incarnation." [4] What is being said is that the office of preaching is vitally related to the content

[1] *The Servant of the Word* (New York: Charles Scribner's Sons, 1942), p. 14.

[2] *Ibid.*, p. 19.

[3] Quoted in Arthur A. Cowan, *The Primacy of Preaching Today* (New York: Charles Scribner's Sons, 1956), p. 4.

[4] F. D. Coggan, *The Ministry of the Word* (London: Canterbury Press, 1946), p. 18.

of our faith. As Cowan has said, "The manner is part of the matter of the sermon." [5]

Rudolf Bultmann enunciates an equally high conception of preaching. In his opinion, the "salvation-occurrence" (i.e., the kerygma) is nowhere present except in the act of preaching. But this is not limited to the New Testament period alone. His existential note brings him to affirm that the "salvation-occurrence" continues to take place in the preaching of the Word.[6] That is, it was not only an historical event which was proclaimed, but in the contemporary world the preaching of this message is also of the nature of a proclamation. P. T. Forsyth held the same view, maintaining that preaching is still both proclamation and content. "With preaching Christianity stands or falls because it is the declaration of a Gospel. . . . It is the Gospel prolonging and declaring itself." [7]

What we see here, then, is an attempt by modern theologians to restate the Reformation doctrine of the primacy of preaching. Assuming the Reformers were right, this is in essence the New Testament conception of preaching as well. Bishop Brilioth's excellent little pamphlet on the history of preaching tends to support this view. He states that the ministry of the New Testament is entrusted to the sound of the living voice. And then in quoting Luther he avers that "the preaching of the Church contains, in all humility, our Lord's own activity." [8]

[5] Cowan, *op. cit.*, p. 109.

[6] *Theology of the New Testament* (New York: Charles Scribner's Sons, 1951), I, 302.

[7] *Positive Preaching and the Modern Mind* (New York: Armstrong and Son, 1907), p. 5.

[8] *Landmarks in the History of Preaching* (London: S.P.C.K., 1950), p. 2.

Bishop Gerald Kennedy, in his book *His Word Through Preaching,* says:

> Not only is it [preaching] a means of spreading information about the Christian faith, but it is in some sense a revelation of that faith in itself. . . . The very act of preaching is a part of the Christian revelation. Though other religions and other movements might dispense with speakers and use some other method of spreading themselves, Christianity could not.[9]

Now obviously these views tend to elevate preaching to the center of the ministry. Such a high view almost makes preaching sacramental. Indeed, a close examination of what one might call the theology of the office of preaching leads to the claim that the actual *message* of the gospel is tied inextricably to the *preaching* of the gospel. For some this may well be too high a conception of preaching; for others it may seem too narrow. Nevertheless, it is fruitful to test this thesis in a brief historical fashion.

A careful reading of the New Testament reveals that preaching is at the heart of its message. The Gospels record from the first pages that John the Baptist came preaching, "Repent, for the kingdom of heaven is at hand" (Matt. 3:2). He was preaching a message proclaiming the inauguration of the Kingdom and urging repentance in order to be ready for that kingdom. Although it is not the purpose here to analyze the theological aspects of his message, it is quite clear that it was a preached or proclaimed message.

[9] (New York: Harper & Row, 1947), p. 9.

And Jesus, too, came preaching. In Matt. 4:17 it says, "From that time Jesus began to *preach,* saying, 'Repent, for the kingdom of heaven is at hand' "; in Mark, "Now after John was arrested, Jesus came into Galilee, *preaching* the gospel of God, and saying, 'The time is fulfilled, and the kingdom of God is at hand; repent, and believe in the gospel' " (1:14-15). And in Luke 4:18-19 there is the significant passage where Jesus stood up in the synagogue and read from Isaiah:

> The Spirit of the Lord is upon me,
> because he has anointed me to *preach* good news
> to the poor.
> He has sent me to *proclaim* release to the captives
> and recovering of sight to the blind,
> to set at liberty those who are oppressed,
> to *proclaim* the acceptable year of the Lord.

Whatever else may be said about Jesus as a teacher, as a man, or as a Savior, it is quite clear that in the Synoptics he is considered—in his earthly ministry—as a preacher. And to simplify his message, one could probably say that the content of his preaching was the reign of God.

But immediately the question arises: Can we consider Jesus a preacher of the gospel when in reality he is himself part of the gospel? Isn't Jesus himself part of the Christian message? Did not the early church preach that Jesus in his life and teaching, but also in his death and resurrection (i.e., kerygma) was the content of the message? It is certainly true that the message of Jesus and that of the early church were not the same, but it is probably unfair to say that they were wholly different. Bultmann is perhaps too strong in stating that "theological thinking did not begin with Jesus but only with the kerygma and Christ was that message."[10] Yet he is undoubtedly accurate when he says, in regard to the preaching of the early church, "The proclaimer became the proclaimed."[11]

It is unfair, however, to place all the eggs in the kerygmatic basket. The historian H. T. Kerr sees this clearly when he states: "While Christian preaching begins at Pentecost, the theme of the preaching of Jesus and that of apostolic preaching is the same. Jesus came preaching the kingdom of God. He announced that the kingdom of God was at hand. After Pentecost the Apostles proclaimed that the kingdom had come."[12] This would tend to support the view of R. W. Dale that while Jesus "came to preach the gospel, His chief object in coming was that there might be a gospel to preach."[13] Jesus was certainly proclaiming the kingdom of God, and it is true that he became part of the preaching of the apostolic church. Yet it is quite clear that Jesus himself was a proclaimer of the gospel, a preacher of the Word of God, and an announcer of the inauguration of God's kingdom.

When we turn from the preaching of Jesus to that of Paul and the early apostolic church, preaching is seen as a full-blown development of what was alluded to earlier. As to the message of preaching, it is clear that Jesus

[10] *Op. cit.*, p. 3.
[11] *Ibid.*, p. 33.
[12] *Preaching in the Early Church* (New York: Fleming H. Revell, 1942), p. 15.
[13] *The Atonement* (London: Congregational Union of England and Wales, 1905), p. 107.

himself had become part of the preached gospel. He was no longer the proclaimer; he was the proclaimed. This was the kerygma—the life and teachings of Jesus, to be sure, but also the death and resurrection. To some scholars like C. H. Dodd, the kerygma was the basis or the entire content of apostolic preaching. In fact, he tends to define preaching solely in kerygmatic terms. Other kinds of public instruction in the church he would call teaching (*didache*). In the revival of interest in preaching today, this distinction has again risen. However, it is unfortuante to make such a rigid distinction. The preaching of the Word is a teaching function of the church with ethical implications. Conversely, the ethical teachings of the Christian church should always be oriented toward and undergirded by the proclamation of Jesus Christ as Savior. Therefore, most modern preachers would find Dodd's distinction a relatively false one. J. B. Weatherspoon believes Dodd's dichotomy is not a true one, even in relation to the Greek text. He feels that the distinction between teaching and preaching is not valid. The proper distinction is between heralding (*kerussein*), or evangelizing (*evangelizesthai*) on the one hand and teaching (*didaskein*) on the other. He contends that there is no one word for preaching. In fact, he argues for at least seven words in the New Testament which would blanket such seemingly diverse meanings as *didache* and *kerussein*.

But he certainly claims that preaching was the task of the disciples in New Testament times. Weatherspoon's thesis is that the very word "apostle" meant preacher. These early leaders of the church were itinerant evangelists who were primarily preachers. In his exact words,

"Their primary business was to proclaim the Gospel. They were sent forth to preach." [14]

It should be clear what Paul's conception of preaching was, both as to content and presentation. "Woe to me if I do not preach the gospel!" (I Cor. 9:16.) "And how are they to believe in him of whom they have never heard? And how are they to hear without a preacher? . . . Faith comes from what is heard, and what is heard comes by the preaching of Christ." (Rom. 10:14, 17.) "We preach Christ crucified, a stumbling-block to Jews and folly to Gentiles." (I Cor. 1:23.) To Paul, as to the other apostles, Jesus Christ became part of the gospel which in turn was a preached Word.

If the importance of preaching can be established in the New Testament and apostolic times, what happened to preaching from the days of the early church to the Reformation? Is it true, as is commonly thought, that as the organized, formal church grew, preaching declined? Or perhaps an even more common question would be: Is it true that as the mass and sacraments predominate, the preaching of the Word recedes? It is commonly believed that during the rise of the Roman church, and especially during the Middle Ages, preaching died until it was resurrected by the Reformers.

There are many problems with such a widely accepted view. For one thing, during the period of the rise of the Church there were many great preachers. It would be difficult to affirm that preaching had declined when we

[14] *Sent Forth to Preach* (New York: Harper & Row, 1954), p. 25.

view the splendor of Chrysostom, Basil, Ambrose, and Augustine, churchmen, to be sure, but all very effective preachers as well. In fact, many of them were known primarily as preachers, even though today we may think of them as theologians or churchmen. Finally, the so-called renaissance of preaching did not begin with the Reformers, but had begun sometime before. Although Luther, *et al.* undergirded preaching with the theology of the Word, its revival and importance were not limited to the Reformation period.

If there is an unfortunate separation today between the sacraments and the office of preaching, it must certainly be found in other places than in the nature of the Word or in the New Testament period. There was no such division in the thinking of the early church. For example, they were so closely allied that in Paul's famous passage in Corinthians (I Cor. 11:26) the two are inseparable. To Paul, the Lord's Supper is a special mode of the Word proclamation. Speaking of the Communion, he says, "For as often as you eat this bread and drink the cup, you *proclaim* the Lord's death until he comes." The significant thing is that the word translated "proclaim" is the same word Paul uses for preaching or proclamation elsewhere. (I Cor. 9:14; Phil. 1:18; Col. 1:28.)

The coupling of proclamation and sacrament seems to be the predominant theme of those who would keep the Protestant-Catholic traditions in proper balance. Karl Barth, who certainly places the preaching of the Word in the center of his theology, nevertheless feels that the sacrament is tied to the preaching of the Word. In fact, he contends that preaching and sacrament are two modes of proclamation. "Jesus Christ has given His Church the commission to proclaim, and to proclaim through preaching and sacrament." [15] Some such dual and co-ordinate statement has become a basic tenet of the Protestant faith. In fact, it might be said that the church itself is defined on the basis of its role as a conservator of preaching and sacrament. As Calvin said, "Whenever we find the Word of God purely preached, and the sacraments administered . . . there is the Church." [16] Similar to this are the creedal statements which embody the same idea. In Article XII of The Methodist Church, the church is defined as "a congregation of faithful men in which the pure Word of God is preached, and the Sacraments duly administered according to Christ's ordinance."

Henry Sloane Coffin, in his excellent little book *Communion Through Preaching,* restates this ancient affirmation for the modern church. "Both sermons and the Supper of the Lord are means of grace and media through which God in Christ offers Himself in personal fellowship." [17] In his view, the overbalance of one of these elements to the neglect of the other is a danger, and a misreading of the Reformers' thought. Coffin, in his belief that the Word and sacrament must be kept together, is enunciating what he considers to be "sacramental" preaching.

Lest one would think that this equation of preaching and the sacrament is strictly a Protestant development, one should hasten to add that many in the Catholic tradi-

[15] *The Doctrine of the Word of God, Church Dogmatics* I/1 (New York: Charles Scribner's Sons, 1955), p. 62.

[16] Quoted in Kerr, *op. cit.*, p. 88.

[17] (New York: Charles Scribner's Sons, 1952), p. vii.

tion feel the same way. It would not be fair to say that this attitude is normative for the Catholic branch of the church, but there are those in that tradition who feel that the preaching of the Word cannot be overlooked. They see the importance of the ministry of the Word as much as the ministry of the sacrament. Fr. Augustine Bea has said, "The priest who is competent only in one and not in both of these ministries is only half a priest." [18] It seems clear that such a plea for balance is not carried out in actual practice. Most Protestants feel that the Catholic tradition—both Roman and Anglican—has neglected the preaching of the Word to the elevation of the sacraments. On the other hand, the Catholics contend that the Protestants have neglected the sacraments in elevating preaching. There is, of course, room for this latter charge. P. T. Forsyth, although considering both the sacraments and preaching important, is very clear as to which one he believes commands the most respect. "The great, the fundamental, sacrament is the Sacrament of the Word." [19] "The preacher's place in the Church is sacramental." [20] "Preaching then is the Church confessing its faith." [21] To him, preaching is the same as reciting a creed—the faith of the church is being proclaimed.

Many Protestants today would want to agree with Forsyth, yet at the same time place the sacraments on a higher level. Perhaps one of the most fitting ways to

[18] Quoted in *Theology,* LX (January, 1957), 4.
[19] *Op. cit.,* p. 6.
[20] *Ibid.,* p. 80.
[21] *Ibid.,* p. 100.

state this would be to say that the sermon itself should be regarded as a sacramental act. In the specific words of Coggan, "At the table of the Lord we hear: 'This is My Body'; at the Pulpit; 'This Is My Word.' "[22] Or, in the epigrammatic words of Bezzel: "The Word is the audible sacrament and sacrament is the visible Word."[23]

What can we say about this high conception of preaching? Is it valid or is it too narrow? Does it make the preaching office too exclusively the way God's truth is mediated?

First of all, this thesis needs restatement today. As was pointed out earlier, it is not a defense of present-day preaching, but rather judgment. Many modern-day pulpits in the evangelical, liberal Protestant communions have departed into far countries, feeding on the husks of relevancy. This has resulted in topical preaching gone berserk. As someone has said, even if a text is used, the text will be from the Bible and the sermon from the newspapers. This re-emphasis on the centrality of the Word of God makes us aware of our responsibility to rediscover the central core of our message, which is what God has done and is doing through the life, teachings, death, and resurrection of our Lord and Savior Jesus Christ.

The re-emphasis upon the Lord's Supper is needed also in most Protestant evangelical churches. Too often it has become an empty ceremony, celebrated weekly or periodi-

[22] *Op. cit.*, p. 92.
[23] Johannes Rupprecht, *Herman Bezzel als Theologe* (1925), p. 369.

cally, with ever decreasing meaning and confusion. Certainly few churches have seen its co-ordinate relationship to the Word proclaimed from the pulpit.

The danger of this re-emphasis on preaching and sacrament is also apparent. Many of our continental brethren tend to see the proclamation of the Word in some sacerdotal or magical sense, as if the repetition of specifically theological words will be efficacious in the salvation process. The preacher's own role is minimized; the concern for communication is denounced; and the Word is seen only in a confessional sense. The problem here is in leaving little or no room for the apologetic task of preaching, or, in considering preaching simply a word to the faithful. In truth, there is no dichotomy between the essential gospel preached within the confession of the church and that preached to the world, but we do need to preach to the world. The language may differ, the approach may vary, and even the message may be recast, for this message is not static. It is not suspended halfway between heaven and earth like Mohammed's coffin, touching neither. Revelation is situational. God revealed himself in a point of time in Christ; he continues to reveal himself in history in a point or points of time. Therefore, the revelation proclaimed must always be made relevant because his Word is meaningless apart from our situation. Therefore, preaching is indeed proclamation today, but it is in the context of events to which the preacher must address himself.

Tillich's method of correlation here speaks to the preacher. In his words, "It [the method] tries to correlate the questions implied in the situation with the answers implied in the message." [24] The preacher, then, stands with one foot in the realm of the gospel and one in his contemporary world. He holds both in tension; he neglects one or the other at his peril.

Another concern of the thesis in today's setting is that the preaching office must be seen through the preacher. Brooks's words, "truth through personality," have relevance here. Preaching is not simply the transference of theological ideas from one mind to another. This gospel message is being revealed through a person, whose own response to it will be a tremendous factor in its transmission. The Word was made flesh *then* and *now.* The sermon is an encounter between preacher and God, God and people, preacher and people, and people and people. The nonrational aspects of the preacher's witness are vital to the message being proclaimed, and the pulpit affords the best setting—within the context of the worship experience, of course—that we have for mediating God's Word.

Finally, it should be pointed out that preaching is not the only way to witness, to transmit, or to mediate the Word of God. There are, of course, other ways. But it is a mistake to degrade the office of preaching because of one of two errors: bad practice of not proclaiming the Word; or, making proclamation a theological formula of words. Both extremes are wrong conceptions. Preaching can be proclamation in the basic sense without being narrowly kerygmatic. Here is another problem with some modern theologians. We mentioned earlier the quarrel

[24] *Systematic Theology* (Chicago: University of Chicago Press, 1951), I, 8.

with Dodd's definition of preaching as solely kerygmatic. All other kinds of instruction he would call *didache*. By his definition, many preachers would not be preaching on Sunday mornings—they would be giving ethical exhortations. Here again the dichotomy is false. Proclamation of the kerygma without ethical implications is irrelevant. Ethical exhortations without the underlying proclamation of the Christ-event is simple moralism. The preacher's task is to be both kerygmatic and relevant.

Therefore, if one takes a high view of preaching, it is not necessarily narrow. Preaching is not in a vacuum. For one example, the most effective kind of preaching in our day might be called pastoral. This concept fits in with Richard Niebuhr's view of the pastor-director, which at first glance seems to minimize the role of preaching. But, according to Niebuhr, the pastor-director does not make preaching less important, but changes the aim from, shall we say, kerygmatic to pastoral. In other words, modern preaching may well tend to be didactic in the broadest sense rather than kerygmatic in the narrow sense.

Yet, no matter how preaching may be defined or categorized, no one can doubt its importance in the Protestant tradition. Robert Michaelson, in the second volume of the Niebuhr report, writes, "Preaching remains perhaps the most dramatic, most effective, and most used means of communicating the gospel in Protestantism and will always be central in a tradition that stresses the primacy of the Word of God." [25] If this is our calling, what a

[25] H. Richard Niebuhr and Daniel D. Williams, eds., *The Ministry in Historical Perspectives* (New York: Harper & Row, 1956), p. 285.

tremendous challenge and what a thrilling responsibility! There is no higher calling, no greater thrill, than to be a proclaimer of God's Word. Although the concept of the preacher as an artist is not an exact comparison, Henry Sloane Coffin has a quotation from Sir Edward Burne-Jones which is suggestive. Burne-Jones summarizes the task of the artist with a statement from John Ruskin that

> artists paint God for the world. There's a lump of greasy pigment at the end of Michelangelo's hog-bristle brush, and by the time it has been laid on the stucco, there is something that all men with eyes recognize as Divine. Think what it means: it is the power of bringing God into the world—making God manifest.[26]

So it is with preaching. We have the honor and responsibility—through God's grace—of bringing God into the world—making God manifest.

[26] Coffin, *op. cit.*, p. 124.

CHAPTER II

Proclaiming the Word Within the Bible: Theory

One of the best-known statements to come out of World War II was made by a chaplain. It was not, "Praise the Lord and pass the ammunition," but, "Gee, I didn't know there were so many sermons in the Bible!" This alarming and facetious statement was made by one who had been trained in the heyday of topical preaching and now, forced to move rapidly and often, could not carry much more than the Bible in the way of books. Too, the war itself forced him to the examination of the essentials of his faith. He had to come to terms with the Bible in a new and vital way. This incident is a parable of the biblical renaissance which has taken place in the last few years, preceding, accompanying, or following after the theological resurgence. Halford E. Luccock put it graphically when he said, speaking of the preachers, "They began to be in want. Then they came to themselves and said,

'In my father's Book are texts enough and to spare.' And they said, 'I will arise and go to the Bible.' "[1]

Although we might admit that there has been a resurgence of interest in the Bible in the last few years, there is no assurance that there is any uniform approach to the use of the Bible or that preaching itself has been improved thereby. For it still remains painfully clear that how we use the Bible in preaching is determined largely by what we believe about the Bible. Our theological position with regard to the authority of the Bible determines its use in preaching. Therefore, the return to the Bible movement along almost all fronts in Christendom is not necessarily a boon to preaching. The first task for the preacher, then, is to come to a theological understanding of and confrontation with the Bible. After this he will be ready to preach from a theological stance and avoid a simple pragmatic use of biblical materials.

The varieties of belief about the Bible can be demonstrated as one looks at the possible platforms on which the preacher can stand. Does he consider the Bible primarily history? If so, this position will determine his use of the Bible in preaching.

Is it literature, as one would view other great books of mankind? If so, his sermons will be affected by this literary interpretation of biblical materials. A few years ago, on the radio program "Invitation to Learning," a group of men including Lyman Bryson and Red Barber were discussing the Psalms. This discussion illustrated the various

[1] *In the Minister's Workshop* (Nashville: Abingdon Press, 1944), p. 149.

points of view which could be taken in regard to the Bible. There was a professor of English Bible, a literary critic, and a sports announcer. The majority were content and determined to discuss the Bible as a book of literature, examining the strophes, stanzas, and literary quality. Only Red Barber seemed concerned to discuss it as a religious book which spoke to him on a deeper level.

Others look at the Bible as a book of science. Or rather, many feel that science must conform to the cosmology and anthropology of the Bible or be declared atheistic. As a child I remember listening to an evangelist, Harry Rimmer, who took pains to point out that the Bible was a book which could be reconciled with science. He declared the earth could have been created in six days as Genesis reports. He avowed that the ark—using the biblical dimensions—could have been built and could have contained all the animals known in the world at that time. To him, the Bible could meet all scientific tests.

Some preachers would accept parts of these views; others would disclaim them. Most Christian preachers, however, want to declare that the Bible is the Word of God for them. But the Word of God is sometimes a verbal shibboleth, unexamined theologically. To say the Bible is the Word of God is to make a specific theological affirmation which needs explication.

When the Revised Standard Version of the Bible was published, it was reported in the newspapers that a young preacher stood in front of his church and burned several copies to show his disgust with this version which had translated certain words in an unacceptable way. Undoubtedly this young man believed the Bible was the Word of God in a verbally inspired, literalistic sense. Of course, many people would agree with the young man's theology without condoning his practice. It could well be that his faith was in *words,* not in *the Word.* He saw the Word of God as synonymous with the Bible, believing that the words themselves are efficacious. Indeed, not only specific words but even specific passages can be cited in sermons as proof texts. The very citation will be authoritative, as when the preacher says, "God has given us eternal life, John 3:16."

At the other extreme are those preachers who declare that the Bible is the Word of God only in the sense that it was written by men who were inspired by God in the same way that Gandhi or Kagawa were inspired. This view arises out of an immanental sense of the Divine which is not dependent upon special revelation. Thus, even great literature other than the Bible can be divinely inspired.

The newer, so-called "biblical" theology has helped us a great deal to see the Bible as the Word of God in a dynamic way. This diverse movement takes the Bible seriously; indeed, it declares that it is truly the Word of God. At the same time, there is a concern for historical-critical problems. This view sees the Bible, not as a book of science, literature, history, but as a book of faith.

It will be evident that the presentation is made from a "confessional" rather than an allegedly neutral standpoint. When dealing with the issue of the ultimate meaning of human life there can be no neutrality. Any questioning or rejection of the biblical faith will be made from another faith-standpoint, not from an impartial consideration of the facts. For the Protestant, faith is reliance upon God's love manifested in Christ; it is personal response—within the Church and guided by the Holy Spirit—to God's Word which is mediated through the Bible.[2]

The ground of argument is shifted away from a rationalistic view of the Book and is concerned with what has been called *Heilsgeschichte*—salvation history. The Bible is seen as a record of God's seeking man, as his revelation to man. The Bible becomes an account of his mighty acts in finding man and redeeming him unto himself. Some focus on the covenant relationship of God and his people recorded in the Old Testament and in the revelation of himself through Christ in the New. Others speak of the Bible as the history of God's redemptive acts, seeing the Bible in dramatic form—the drama of God's relationship to man. Such biblical scholars are not afraid of the seeming inconsistencies within the Bible, nor are they alarmed by the so-called higher criticism. Indeed, they welcome such study. For by the assertion that the Bible is divine in revealing God's will to man, it becomes the book of faith for the covenanted people—then and now.

This group of men affirm that the Bible is the Word of God in the highest sense possible. They do not, however, confuse *word* with *Word*. They conceive of the Word of God as conversation between two friends where the language is not so important as the person and idea transmitted. They see the Bible arising in historical situations

[2] Bernhard W. Anderson, *Rediscovering the Bible* (New York: Association Press, 1951), p. ix.

where God addressed men. As Anderson puts it, "The 'Word of God' was essentially the interpretation of historical crisis in which men were grasped by God's claim upon them." [3] The Word of God cannot be identified with the Bible, nor are the literal words his words. The Word of God is the Word behind the words. It is the creative act of God—in his world, in Christ, in his relationship to men—and revealed in the Bible. "It is inaccurate to speak of the Bible itself as the Word of God. Properly speaking, the Bible contains the Word of God." [4] No one would consider Luther a historical critic, yet even he speaks of the Bible as the manger in which the Christ child is laid. So it is with the Word of God. It is not the Bible; it is found there.

This brings us to another important point. It is found there when it claims us. This is perhaps the most important step of all. For the words of the Bible to become the Word of God to us, they must confront us in a personal, existential way. The Bible becomes God's Word for us when he claims us through its words. The writers were not dispassionate men; they wrote in the white heat of faith. When we are confronted personally by that faith through worship, study, prayer, and hearing the Word read and preached, the Word of God then speaks to us a very personal word. For us, then, it becomes the Word of God. The preacher's primary task is to communicate this Word found in the Bible so that it may become personal history to the congregation. If this is what preaching is, then it

[3] *Ibid.*, p. 21.
[4] *Ibid.*

follows that Christian preaching is primarily biblical preaching.[5]

If there is confusion in the minister's understanding of the Bible, then it only follows—and usually for the same reason—that there should be confusion in the pulpit as to what is biblical preaching. One cannot quarrel with the amount of Bible used in the pulpits. This has always been the case in some denominations, and the biblical renaissance has invaded other denominations where the Bible has never been prominent in preaching. However, there is still no assurance that the widespread use of the Bible means that it is being preached adequately. A definition of biblical preaching will have more meaning if we look first at some of the prevailing pulpit practices. The word "practice" is used deliberately to denote that, for many ministers, preaching is a pragmatic affair unencumbered with theological undergirding.

The first great group of American preachers we must consider are those who might be called "topical" preachers. Someone might want to use liberal, but that is a theological term which might cause reactions keeping us off the course. The "topical" preacher is one who week by week preaches on Christian themes both from the Bible and from other places. It might be suggested that some topical preachers never use the Bible, so why discuss them? But they, in fact, are saying something about both their theological understanding of the Bible and their concept of its

[5] *Biblical* preaching means *scriptural* preaching. Both are generic terms for proclaiming the Word of God in the Bible. Exposition, textual, and other type biblical sermons are *methods* of biblical or scriptural preaching.

use in the pulpit. Most topical preachers do use the Bible, and many of them will even be upset to see themselves described as topical preachers when they think of themselves otherwise.

The method of the topical preacher varies, but usually it is a completed sermon in search of a text. The preacher writes the sermon, thumbs through a concordance to find an appropriate text, and then affixes the text to the sermon and calls it a biblical sermon, even though there is no serious endeavor to give an exegesis or exposition of the scripture. Sometimes the preacher even leaves off the text entirely, but reads a passage of scripture as a lesson which remains unexamined throughout the sermon but which reflects or gives the background for the theme of the sermon. This practice is really not using texts, but pretexts; it is running the text up the mast or, to change the figure, jacking up the sermon and running a text under it. Since there is no endeavor to examine the passage with any seriousness, this kind of preaching cannot be considered biblical preaching. When a sermon is labeled "biblical," it certainly ought to be biblical.

John C. Irwin, a distinguished professor of preaching, dramatizes admirably this pseudobiblical preaching in an analysis of a sermon in *The Pulpit.*[6] He speaks of having heard a sermon on the subject, "The Art of Growing Old." The sermon revealed careful preparation and good material. After an arresting introduction, the preacher said, "The text for our thought is a word from the ninetieth psalm:

[6] "Some Thoughts on Biblical Preaching," *The Pulpit,* XXIII, 9 (September, 1952).

So teach us to number our days
that we may give our hearts unto wisdom."

Following this, the preacher asserted that the Christian faith provides resources for growing older: i.e., to accept the fact of change; to face the future without worry; to mature inwardly as we grow outwardly; and to realize that increasing age brings compensations. All this material was illustrated and supported. The minister then concluded by quoting Browning and Markham and said, "Thus, with the psalmist, let us so number our days that we may give our hearts unto wisdom."

Irwin asserts rightly that this sermon was not biblical, even though the preacher used a text both in the beginning and at the end of the sermon. The points of the outline were not derived from the passage, and the support did not come from the psalmist's insights. The sermon could just as well have been preached without the text. Even more important, although the sermon may be very good in its own right, there are several consequences from this kind of preaching. One, the preacher may delude himself through the years that he is doing serious biblical preaching. He can look at his sermons and see texts on all of them and convince himself that he is unfolding the contents of the Bible. Two, he is also deluding his people. When they hear a text read each Sunday, they may be tempted to believe that what the preacher is saying is an attempt to exposit that text. In short, the minister is fooling his people and is withholding from them the truths of the Bible which should be the foundation of their faith. As Irwin suggests, a biblical parenthesis at the beginning and end of a topical sermon does not make for biblical preaching.

Although the "topical-biblical" preacher categorizes a host of American preachers, those at the other end of the continuum are equally faulty in their use of the Bible in preaching. These are the so-called "Bible" preachers who are found in abundance in our Protestant evangelical pulpits. These are they whose churches base their faith solely on the Bible, and these preachers consider themselves as preaching *only* the Bible. Although one might be tempted to use the term "fundamentalist," it is not entirely accurate. Fundamentalism is a theological term, and does not adequately describe this method of preaching. There are those who would disclaim the term "fundamentalist" but at the same time affirm their allegiance to the Bible as the basis of their preaching.

Two or three years ago a student preacher from such a church finished his sermon, and was most chagrined to find that the major criticism of the class was that his sermon was not biblical. This was, to him, the most devastating criticism which could be laid against him. Nevertheless, he had preached a rational sermon; i.e., his outline was not derived from the Scripture, but was of his own creation on various ways of faith. True, he used a lot of biblical material to support his points. In fact, he even used passages from many areas of the Bible to proof-text his statements. Yet, his main insights were not biblically derived, and the class was right in leveling the charge that the sermon was not biblical. The basic insights of the sermon were not developed from the Bible in any specific or meaningful way.

In the same discussion, a Disciple student volunteered the insight that Alexander Campbell was affected as much by John Locke as he was by the New Testament, and this had thereby conditioned his progeny among both the Disciples of Christ and the Churches of Christ. The young man was probably too critical and too sweeping in his evaluations; nevertheless, many of our evangelical denominations, including not only the Disciples and the Churches of Christ, but the Methodists, Baptists, Presbyterians, and others which flourished in the nineteenth century, are far more indebted to American rationalism than they would often care to admit. Essentially this means in sermon methodology that the idea, outline, and structure are designed, thought out, or superimposed by the preacher. The preacher then uses the Bible as a textual motto, much as does the topical preacher, or else he profusely uses it for support material and proof texting, often ranging widely over the Bible with little specific attention to one passage. Or, if the Bible is used as the basis of the sermon, with perhaps even the outline deriving from a text quite woodenly, it is often unexegeted, and the sermon does not rest on the biblical insight of the text or passage which in essence determines the nature of biblical preaching.

A third group which causes some problem in regard to biblical preaching is, strangely enough, the group which has spurred the biblical-theological renaissance. This group is made up of a variety of biblical theologians—or rather, their disciples. One might be tempted to call this preaching tendency "neo-orthodoxy," but here again the category does not fit exactly. Many preachers of all theological persuasions have been affected by the biblical revival, and are attempting to utilize the Bible as never before in their preaching. The homiletical methodology of these preachers is to preach *biblical ideas*. They have studied their Bibles, and especially the books on biblical theology. They are excited about the Bible once again, and especially its message. Indeed, they may even be good biblical students. In their preaching, however, they are tempted to preach biblical ideas apart from any specific biblical text or passage. They may take some of the great themes of the Bible; i.e., the covenant people, the redemptive community, the mighty acts of God, and preach these—using various biblical materials as support—apart from any specific locus. The temptation here is to make of the Bible a book of systematic theology, preaching biblical themes sometimes even apart from the Bible itself. This method assumes that the Christian faith has some great affirmations derived from the Bible—as indeed it does—which if preached would guarantee genuinely biblical preaching. But do they? Such preaching may not open up the Bible itself to the people—or for that matter to the preacher himself. Such preaching is deductive, moving from a theme, albeit biblical, and then seeking—if at all—some biblical materials as examples to illustrate the theme.

In short, preaching biblical *ideas* is not the definition of a biblical sermon. Undoubtedly, all Christian sermons should in some way express biblical ideas. Whether or not there can be a Christian sermon apart from biblical ideas or specific texts is a matter that we must deal with later, but at this time we can affirm that a biblical sermon must be more closely related to the specific contents of the

Bible than a general definition of "biblical preaching as preaching biblical *ideas*" would allow.

After considering what biblical preaching is not, we are now ready to consider what a specific definition of biblical preaching is. *Biblical preaching is the proclamation of the kerygma (either explicitly or implicitly) through the exposition of specific scriptural material directed to contemporary life.* There are three basic affirmations in this definition which should be in all sermons which purport to be biblical.

First, the biblical sermon should proclaim the kerygma, either explicitly or implicitly. The kerygma is the kernel of the Christian gospel: the life, teachings, death, and resurrection of Jesus Christ. Whether it is called the kerygma, the Christ-event, or the "salvation-occurrence," it is this proclamation which makes preaching distinctively Christian. A sermon which lacks this proclamation may be good advice, but it is seldom good news. A sermon without the proclamation of what God has done and continues to do in Christ will be moralistic and humanistic. Indeed, not only in preaching, but in theology itself, we can see the difficulties when one aspect of the kerygma is neglected or overemphasized. Some preachers emphasize the life and teachings; others, the death and Resurrection. But the Christian gospel is the total event of what God has done in Christ. "God was in Christ, reconciling the world unto himself." (K.J.V.) This includes not only his life and teachings, but also his death and resurrection. It presents us not only with the Law, but with the gospel; it presents us not only with the Example, but with the Savior; it presents us not only with an "ought," but with the power and motivation to respond and follow. Christian preaching is, in a sense, telling the old, old, story—over and over again.

Of course, this kerygmatic proclamation will need not be explicit in every sermon. Every sermon will not have to end with a verbal statement of the kerygma which would equate verbal affirmation with belief. It need not be dragged in as a theological formulation which gives the sermon Christian validity. Further, it need not be an excuse to baptize every Old Testament sermon or to seek out christological inferences in every verse in the Old Testament. It may remain silent as a verbal statement, but remain real as the framework within which the sermon gains validity as a Christian sermon. Even though it remains silent, it is the culmination of our Old Testament preaching and the heart of our New. Whether expressed or not, it is the capstone of our preaching, the underlying assumption of every sermon, and the *raison d'être* for our calling.

Second, the biblical sermon will be the exposition of *specific* scriptural material. Whereas preaching biblical ideas is *deductive* preaching, true biblical preaching is *inductive*. It begins with specific scripture and finds there the source of the sermon. While some biblical preaching uses texts as mottoes or pretexts, this method really examines the scripture passage. While some preaching announces a text, and even uses much biblical material to support an imposed outline, this method lets the sermon develop from the passage studied. The advantages here are apparent. This method endeavors to let the Bible speak. It seeks to make the preacher study his Bible and thus educate his people as his sermons develop from the Scripture.

At first glance, preaching from specific biblical material may suggest the method of our grandfathers in dealing with the dimensions of Solomon's temple, and therefore a rather wooden examination of the Bible for its own sake. It is true that the Bible is examined specifically, but as we shall see when we look at the method of building such a biblical sermon, the sermon never stays with a specific passage. It begins there, bringing to bear all the exegetical tools of the minister's study, but then moves out to its meaning in a larger context, the meaning within the book, the theological meaning underlying the passage, its relationship to the kerygmatic proclamation, and finally, its relevance to our day and time. It takes the Bible seriously as the data for our faith, beginning with its words, letting the Word speak through them, and moving in concentric circles right into our present lives.

The third aspect of the definition is that biblical preaching is directed to meeting the needs of contemporary life. This emphasis is necessary to take biblical materials out of the past and bring them into our present lives. Indeed, this is exactly what the prophets did with their own faith. This keeps biblical preaching from being a recounting of the past, as if there is something magical in using these records as simply records. This emphasis believes that the Word speaks through the words and becomes our present history. The Word is never entombed in the Bible, but becomes alive through it as it possesses our own lives in the here and now. The preacher has the task of "demythologizing" the message, freeing it from the historical encrustations and letting it come alive to the people whom he addresses. But to do so, he must hear the Word as it speaks through the words of the Bible. Therefore, he must become a faithful student and perennial expositor of the Scriptures. But he must see, as the biblical writers saw, that the gospel is contemporaneous. It is God's Word speaking to us now. The gospel is incarnational. God was in Christ, reconciling the *world* unto himself. It is present history, and so must be adapted to meet the needs of our time. No one can tell the preacher to "stick to the Bible" and "stay out of social and political affairs" and use the Bible as his authority. On the contrary, the Bible is concerned exactly with interpreting God's will to the present day—then and now. True biblical preaching can be scriptural only when it develops a message from its source that can be proclaimed to the people in a relevant way.

Biblical preaching is the attempt to open up again the pages of the Bible to the twentieth century. It seeks to share the words of the Scripture through which the Word speaks and apprehends modern man in a timely and meaningful way. Biblical preaching confronts modern man with the gospel through its source—the Bible—and demonstrates the claim upon him to respond to God's call in Christ, a call that comes relevantly to him in the present day.

CHAPTER III

Proclaiming the Word Within the Bible: Method

It should be obvious that the preacher must be a faithful student of the Bible in order to proclaim the Word found there. A good case could be made that never in the history of our seminaries has there been such good Bible instruction. The teachers of today are excellent biblical students and at the same time theologians. Thus, the average graduate has studied with devout men who are committed to the Book and at the same time are critical scholars in the best sense of that word.

The average preacher studies the Bible but fails to employ his methodology for study to the building of the sermon; and as we have seen, it is because he is often confused as to the nature of a biblical sermon. His task is to come to some understanding of the nature of biblical preaching and then to set himself to that task in the study. For this latter reason, it is our purpose here to examine the steps involved in building a biblical sermon predicated on the definition given in the last chapter. His methods of Bible study may be good. He has simply made a false dichotomy between the methods used in classroom biblical study and sermon preparation, or else he has an incorrect concept of biblical preaching.

Let us assume for a moment that the preacher is in his study, and has before him a specific passage of scripture or a text which will be the basis of his next Sunday's sermon. What are the steps he takes in unfolding the meaning of the scripture? First, he should get inside this scripture, to see what the writer intended. What was the author trying to say? What was the original meaning here? What truth about the gospel and what meaning for me is the Holy Spirit trying to convey in this passage? These, or similar questions, are the goals to be attacked in approaching the scripture before him. The preacher is to come to this passage—no matter how familiar it may be—with as little prejudice as possible. He is to divest himself of all preconceptions, all desires to read into it a sermon he already has in mind, and all temptations to make a twentieth-century adaptation. Of course, it is impossible to come to scripture completely *de novo,* but nevertheless that is the preacher's goal.

We are suggesting that the preacher's task is an exegetical one. Just as he may have learned to exegete a passage in his classroom study, he must carry over that same task to the preaching ministry in preparing a biblical sermon. As Americans, we feel somewhat dismayed by exegesis because we usually associate it with language study; and many of us do not feel equipped to read our Bibles in the original, let alone make a detailed study of the historical and linguistic backgrounds of the biblical passages. Yet exegesis need not be so forbidding, even for those bound by the English texts. For not only do we have fine biblical texts in English; we have commentaries, dictionaries, and other aids which enable us to unlock the biblical passages' meanings.

Exegesis comes from the Greek verb meaning to expound or to interpret. The preacher is to seek the meaning of and expound the passage before him. To unlock the meaning of the passage, we are brought to the steps in exegesis that a preacher may have studied in seminary, but that are laid away when he preaches. Let him consider them again as he sits before the scripture passage.

This first step is to make a lexical study of the words in the text or passage which need clarification. The preacher needs to understand the words given in any specific passage in their historical, doctrinal, biblical setting. Of course, every word will not need this intensive investigation, but certainly the key words will have to be properly understood. He cannot assume he knows the theological meaning of even the religious terminology which is his stock and trade. Each text must be apprehended anew with every sermon. Take for example a great text like "God was in Christ reconciling the world to himself" (II Cor. 5:19). There are several terms in this familiar text which the preacher should understand thoroughly if he is to preach the text intelligently. He must seek the original meaning of the author. "God" and "Christ" are of course familiar, but what did Paul mean by "God was in Christ" or "in Christ God was"? This raises the question of Pauline christology, and the preacher should get that firmly in mind before he attempts to preach on this text. Or, for another example, take the word "reconcile," probably the key word in this passage. What does *reconcile* mean? A dictionary answer is not enough. Reconciliation is a significant Pauline term, and no cursory rendering of this term will suffice. The preacher will be led from this text through most of the Pauline letters, seeking this term in its various contexts. He will be involved in the comparisons of the various translations of this text and other similar ones which deal with reconciliation. He will go to Bible dictionaries, commentaries, and various word books to seek to understand Paul's meaning.

If the preacher can handle the Greek text, so much the better; but if not, he can use Kittel's *Theologisches Wörterbuch,* or *Bible Key Words,* Coates's Interpretation of Kittel's dictionary. Such terms as church, faith, love, spirit of God, sin, and righteousness have been translated. These or books such as Alan Richardson's *Theological Wordbook of the Bible* and *The Interpreter's Dictionary of the Bible* are indispensable tools for the preacher who would seek the biblical meaning of key words. Such a word as "reconcile" would need this painstaking examination.

After the preacher has examined the key words in his passage or text in this thorough manner, he is now ready for the next step; that is, he should examine the word in its sentence. This is a syntactical examination—its grammatical setting. How does the grammar of a sentence affect its meaning? (A good example would be Job 13:15, which in the King James is: "Though he slay me, yet will I trust in him: but I will maintain mine own ways before him." But the RSV translates the passage: "Behold, he will slay me; I have no hope; yet I will defend my ways to his face." In this instance, a grammatical as well as a theological understanding would be imperative for the preacher dealing with this text.) The tense of a verb; whether or not a noun is possessive; what is the object of the verb—all these grammatical questions may vitally affect the meaning of a text. This is part and parcel of the task of the exegete.

The third step concerns the words in their context. The text should be seen in its larger setting. What was the purpose, time, and setting of the text or passage? I once heard a preacher using as his scripture the parable of the sower. He began by discussing the pastoral nature of the Palestinian setting and how natural it was for Jesus to be standing in the midst of these tillers of soil and uttering the parable of the sower. Actually this parable was delivered from a boat, and the people stood on the beach (Matt. 13). In this instance, no more harm was done than to show the inadequacy of the preacher's study, but in many cases the context would have a direct and important bearing on the meaning of the passage itself.

The fourth step concerns the passage in its historical setting. This is similar to the last step of context, only here the preacher is concerned with the immediate situation, the customs, manners, and mores of a people. It is an understanding of the writer and those for whom it was written. Such a book as John's Gospel affords a good example. When written? Why? To whom? For what purpose? These questions are not sterile, but are vital to preaching on a passage in the book. If the Gospel of John was not written as a biography in the usual sense, but rather as a document designed to portray Jesus as the eternal Logos, then each passage in that book should be seen in that light.

The last step for the exegesis of a passage of scripture concerns the passage in terms of the total biblical viewpoint. For those who might feel that the exegesis of a specific passage is too wooden, or too inductive, or too limited to one passage, then here is the answer. The passage is always seen finally in its larger setting—the biblical viewpoint. If, for example, Mark's Gospel leaves something to be desired as a factual biography of Jesus (i.e., the absence of Jesus' birth and lineage, such as in Matthew and Luke), then it must be remembered that Mark assumed much of what we would call biographical facts. He was concerned to show that Jesus was the Son of God. His teachings, his healings, his activities are all demonstrations of the mighty acts of God in Christ. Each text in Mark must be seen through this prism. And Mark itself will be seen in the total biblical view, which by and large is the Christology taken over and promulgated by the Christian church.

Now, after these steps are completed—and only then—the preacher is ready to ask the question, What is the bearing or relevance of this passage for our day, faith, and life? This last question cannot be answered adequately until the former questions have been answered. Of course, all will not necessarily come out in the sermon. Much of the minister's exegesis will and should remain in his study. But the point is clear: a biblical preacher must subject himself to the kind of discipline which enables him to unlock the meaning of the passages before him. Only when he has done this basic biblical study should the homiletician in him take over. After he has discerned the meaning of the scripture, then he is ready to make it relevant to contemporary life. To try to preach biblically without this basic exegesis is like a surgeon entering an operating room without a scalpel. The preacher can only be a relevant Christian preacher when he knows the basis of his faith—the Bible. Anything less than this kind of devotion may end up as interesting discourses, entertaining speeches, or helpful moralistic homilies, but it will not be biblical preaching unless the preacher pays the price of dedicated work in the study.

We now turn to the form that the biblical sermon may take as the homiletician in the minister takes over from the student. What are the best ways to present the biblical material in the pulpit? One must be very careful here. It is easy to be dogmatic and lay down certain set forms, one of which all biblical material will fit. But such a rigidity does not take into account the creativity and preferences of the individual preacher. "Each star differs in its glory," and nowhere is that more apparent than in the various preaching methods. Too, it is difficult to superimpose forms and outlines on scripture material. This practice makes preaching wooden, rigid, and sterile. To wed oneself to certain patterns of handling biblical material is like screening coal, in that one shakes the material over certain holes until the particular passage falls through one of the forms which the preacher habitually uses. Above all, effective form comes from the idea itself. The idea—the biblical material—should have locked within it its own form and outline. Part of the creative task of the preacher is to develop, unlock, or see the form take shape as he wrestles with the passage and its idea. One pattern may work one time, another the next. The individual preacher will experiment, find his own method, change and revise, listen to others, and, above all, be attentive to the biblical material in front of him. If he has this dedication and discipline, then the form of presentation will come as part of the whole creative enterprise of building a sermon.

Nevertheless, it is helpful for illustrative purposes to look at some of the ways in which a biblical sermon may unfold. These are not presented as the ways in which biblical material *must* be used; they are examples of how it *can* be used. Each preacher could, and probably should, add or subtract from the list.

The most familiar type of biblical sermon—although not necessarily in number of times preached—is the *expository* sermon. It is the most easily recognized, but seemingly difficult for many preachers to use. A strict definition is not important. A preacher cannot proclaim a definition. For our purposes here, it is enough to suggest that an expository sermon deals with a larger portion of scripture than is usually considered in a textual sermon. The expository sermon may deal with a parable, a chapter, a book, or a biblical theme. Assuming that the preacher has a passage before him, what is the best way to develop it?

One of the least complicated and most effective ways to develop an expository sermon is through the following familiar three-point pattern or some variation of it:

I. SETTING
II. MEANING
III. RELEVANCE

There is no more effective way of presenting biblical material than through some such simple development. We hasten to add what should be obvious: that an outline does not make a sermon, nor should a static outline be superimposed upon a man's material, oblivious to the idea itself. The form grows from within the idea, and of course there is no technique that can make a homiletical silk purse out of a lazy preacher's sow's ear. The preacher is the key, along with the Holy Spirit, in effective preaching. Yet, given these indispensable elements of the preacher's task, the recognition that a man does not have to be complex in order to be effective can be of tremendous help. It should not be thought that simplicity in preaching is to be equated with simplemindedness. It is still patently true in preaching, as in other art forms, that great art is disarming in its simplicity. While it would be difficult to state invariable laws in this realm, it does appear that the really effective preachers are marked by simplicity of idea, simplicity of development, and simplicity of language. Profundity and simplicity are not antithetical categories.

Such an outline as we are describing can well be the form which any number of expository sermons could take. A sermon on the book of Jonah, for example, might well spend the first point giving a brief but arresting treatment of the details of the book. The second point might well emphasize the lesson of inclusiveness versus exclusiveness, the concept of the Hebrew God being universal in nature; and then the material could be applied and adapted to our own times in a great many obvious and helpful ways drawn from the thesis of the message. One could do the same with the thirteenth chapter of I Corinthians, with the parable of the good Samaritan, or with practically any other biblical incident that comes to mind. And how true it seems to be that people continue to respond gladly to such treatment of biblical materials.

Another helpful way of developing biblical material expositorily is through a parallel development which takes the basic ideas from the scripture (the points being either derived directly from the scripture, including language; or the points derived from the scripture, but put in the preacher's own words) and develops them in a then-and-now manner. For example, we might take a passage such as Isaiah's vision in the Temple (Isa. 6:1-8).

I. VISION (vss. 1-3)
  A. Isaiah
  B. Us
II. CONFESSION (vss. 4-5)
  A. Isaiah
  B. Us
III. REDEMPTION (vss. 6-7)
  A. Isaiah
  B. Us
IV. DEDICATION (vs. 8)
  A. Isaiah
  B. Us

This is a sample outline for developing a sermon on the theological and psychological pattern of true worship.[1] *A* in each point would be the exposition of the scripture and what this experience meant to Isaiah in his time. *B*

[1] Dr. Sperry developed a pattern of worship from this passage in Isaiah. Willard L. Sperry, *Reality in Worship* (New York: The Macmillan Company, 1925), p. 282.

would be the relevant adaptation to ourselves. This outline has the advantage of getting the relevant section in almost immediately as the sermon develops, as over against the earlier example of a sermon on Jonah, where the twentieth-century adaptation comes near the end of the sermon.

In some ways it is unfortunate to suggest a dichotomy between exegesis or scripture and relevance. This seems to admit that the scriptural exposition is not relevant in itself. On the contrary, if the scripture is handled effectively, then there is relevance aplenty in the very act of unfolding its meaning. The people will hear, understand, and appropriate it for themselves. Relevance, as used here, concerns more the step of adaptation, which is designed to dramatize the scriptural truth in the lives of the listeners. In so doing, we are not depreciating the effectiveness of exegesis; we are merely emphasizing that the truth should be made vivid in the congregation's realm of experience. Such dramatization is the wellspring of response and commitment.

Another method of presenting biblical material, which illustrates the above point, would be the type of sermon that weaves the adaptation in with the exposition, or else spells out the exposition so clearly that the adaptation to our needs is clearly implied. Such a pattern often causes a rather stringy structure, but it can be tremendously effective.

A sermon by one of my colleagues, the distinguished New Testament professor Kendrick Grobel, provides an excellent example. Grobel preached this sermon to a seminary chapel audience; but its method, if not content, would be appropriate in any worship setting. The title was "Living Slaughter," and the passage was the twelfth chapter of Romans, especially verses 1 and 2. This might be considered under the textual type as well, but since he covered much of the message of Paul in Romans and dealt with the passage specifically before him in a detailed word-study manner, it fits our purposes to examine it here. The theme of the sermon concerns priestliness as Paul meant it. The preacher considers each significant word in the two verses. While it is impossible to give the whole sermon, an example of how a word is treated gives the idea of how effective exposition and twentieth-century relevance are combined. Take the verb "present" from the passage "to *present* your bodies as a living sacrifice":

"Present" by itself is not necessarily sacrificial (Mrs. Jones is not sacrificed to Mrs. Smith when she is presented to her—at least, not intentionally!), but "present" coupled in the same phrase with "sacrifice" is unmistakably sacrificial language. But is it the presentation by a layman to a priest, for him to sacrifice? Or is it the actual presentation by the priest on the altar to God? It could be either, but the word used for "service" (KJ) settles the matter. Paul chooses none of his ordinary words for "service" (not even *diakonia,* holy service-to-the-needy, at first by every Christian, and then specifically by the *diakonos*)*;* instead he uses the word reserved (in Jewish Greek) for one use only: the bloody serving of the Jerusalem altar: *thysia.* Therefore "present" is here a synonym for "offer" or "sacrifice"—but either word in its harsh, full, original meaning (not the "offering" that is the dime in your pocket that won't buy much of anything anyway; not the "sacrifice"—that is the giving up of goodies during Lent!), for look *what* you, as priest, are urged to sacrifice: no less than your very self! Don't try to squeeze out from that frightening thought by saying, Oh but it says "bodies," not "selves,"—so doesn't this mean only "mortify the flesh," leaving me my soul and my spirit unsacrificed and so still mine? No! Paul is no dualist. With Hebrew eyes he sees man whole and as a whole: man is body; man is soul; man is spirit; not by addition but by instantaneous photography at three particular perspectives. When Paul says "body" he is just as surely speaking of a whole person as the folk song is of two whole persons when we sing, "If a body meet a body———" This understanding of our passage is beautifully caught up in the Invocation prayer of the Communion service in the Book of Common Prayer (retained in the Methodist Ritual of the Lord's Supper): "And here we offer and present unto thee, O Lord, our *selves,* our *souls* and *bodies,* to be a reasonable, holy, and living sacrifice unto thee." Those are not wilfull additions but proper and necessary interpretations of the true meaning.

Not every preacher would desire to bring as much of the lexical study into the pulpit as did Grobel, but this sermon represents exegesis at its best, permeated by relevance to the listener.

One other type of "biblical" sermon needs to be mentioned. This is the allegorical sermon, which deals figuratively with biblical material. Even though this method of biblical interpretation has a long and hallowed history in preaching (i.e., being used extensively by the early Church Fathers), it is highly debatable whether it should really be called scriptural today. It is difficult to state categorically that the interpretation of scripture fitted for one age is not appropriate for another. Before the advent of historical-critical methods, allegorical interpretations were of undoubted value in opening the Scriptures to the people. Besides, it was a method of interpretation then in vogue for other kinds of literature, and became easily appropriated by the Christians. The key to whether allegory is acceptable concerns the interpretation one has of the Bible. In light of the discussion in the last chapter as to the nature of biblical belief, it will be seen that the allegorical method is usually the church's interpretation of a passage; or rather, the passage is used to point up some already established doctrine of the church. A good example is a sermon by the Venerable Bede (672-735) on Luke 5:

And he saw two ships drawn up by the side of the lake (5:2).

The two ships by the side of the lake represent the circumcised and the uncircumcised. . . .

The fishermen, however, had disembarked, and were washing their nets (5:2).

The fishermen are the teachers of the Church, who gather us together in the net of faith and lift us up out of the depths into the light, like fish upon the shore, and thus bring us to the land of the living. . . .

Going up into one of the ships, that was Simon's, he asked him to push out a little from the shore. And sitting down, he taught the people from the boat (5:3).

The ship of Simon is the Early Church. . . .

When he had finished speaking, he said to Simon: Put out to sea, and let down your nets for the catch (5:4).

The fact that first he asked Simon to put out the ship a little way from the land signifies that the Gospel ought to be preached with moderation to the people. . . . Or [it may signify] that the Gospel should first be preached to the peoples of near-by regions.[2]

Although such allegorical interpretations are fresh, arresting, and often highly imaginative, it is difficult to consider them as serious biblical preaching if the criterion for such preaching is to understand what the passage is really saying and then to apply it to our present day.

The other clear-cut type of biblical sermon is textual. Unlike the expository sermon, the textual sermon usually concerns itself with a verse or so—a text. As was seen in the last chapter, many preachers use texts on their sermons, but they often remain largely unexamined in any meaningful way. Yet the textual type is a hallowed way of dealing with biblical material.

Some theorists define textual preaching as a sermon which gets its structure from a text. Thus, such a verse as "Jesus said, 'I am the way, and the truth, and the life' " would result in the following form:

I. I AM THE WAY
II. I AM THE TRUTH
III. I AM THE LIFE

Such a pattern—although classic and acceptable—should not exhaust the ways a verse may be treated in a scriptural manner. The verse may take the preacher in another direction and still remain textual. One can treat a verse as a whole; that is, instead of unfolding the material in a rigid way prescribed by verse divisions, the preacher may elect to construct another outline than the one the verse obvi-

[2] Quoted in Ray C. Petry, ed., *No Uncertain Sound* (Philadelphia: The Westminster Press, 1948), pp. 104-5.

ously dictates. It would be possible, for example, to consider the same verse in the following manner:

I. WHAT DID OTHERS THINK OF JESUS?
II. WHAT DID JESUS THINK OF HIMSELF?
 A. The Way
 B. The Truth
 C. The Life
III. WHAT DO *WE* THINK OF JESUS?

In this example the preacher has developed the pattern for the sermon, but he is within his right as long as the sermon ideas grow and develop from the passage before him.

Another example of fine textual treatment is a sermon by Harry Emerson Fosdick called "Finding God in Unlikely Places." [3] He states that most of us think of finding God in life's lovely experiences, and feel that God is not in our darkness and disasters. But Moses' experience in the wilderness provides testimony to the fact that God is found in tough places, too. He treats the text "The place on which you are standing is holy ground" (Exod. 3:5) in an imaginative way which reveals careful understanding of the text and a relevant adaptation to our times.

The key to textual preaching, as indeed to all biblical preaching, is not the pattern but the treatment. Does the preacher really make an attempt to exegete the passage—to discover the original meaning of the scripture? When he does this, then he is free to develop the material as he sees fit, remembering one thing—that the idea and development of the sermon (whether or not the structure and language of the verse are used) should evolve from the

[3] In *The Pulpit,* XXIV, 10 (October, 1953), 4-7.

passage itself. A good question to ask is, Could this sermon have been preached without the text? If so, then there should be grave doubts raised as to whether it is biblical or not.

Another type of textual sermon is the text which raises a topic. Such a text is the one used earlier in another connection, "God was in Christ reconciling the world to himself." This text raises the topic of reconciliation. If the preacher stays with that concept within the biblical framework, then there is no reason to doubt that the sermon would and could remain biblical in the truest sense. Many texts, however, do not seem to give enough context to be treated biblically; that is, the exegesis is limited by one verse wrenched out of context. A sermon was once delivered on the text: "Have this mind among yourselves, which you have in Christ Jesus" (Phil. 2:5). The preacher speculated from this text as to what were the marks of Jesus' mind: an open mind, a clear mind, etc. Apart from the fact that theologically and biblically these qualities are not derived from the text, there was no serious attempt to exegete this text to discover its true meaning. Although the text raised the topic, it could not be called a biblical sermon. This particular sermon could have been delivered without any text at all. This is no moral judgment; it might have been a good sermon. It just cannot be called a biblical one.

Often a sermon will use a text in a figurative way. A sermon on Acts 1:9, "And when he had said this, as they were looking on, he was lifted up, and a cloud took him out of their sight," dealt with the ascension of Jesus. After introducing the text, it raised the question, "What are the clouds which take Jesus out of our sight? Pride, prejudice, etc." Although this may be considered a fresh, interesting, and arresting way to handle Scripture, it cannot be considered scriptural unless there is some serious attempt to deal with the scripture at hand. Using some phrase in the verse out of context may be considered imagination at work, but it is hardly an attempt to deal seriously with the meaning of the scripture.

It should be obvious by this time that occasionally a sermon will be hard to classify. A textual sermon may be so close to a topical treatment that the distinctions become blurred. What then? The answer to that is simple: the preacher should not preach *types* of sermons, only sermons themselves. He should be faithful to the text before him, try to understand its original meaning, permit the sermon to develop from it, make it as relevant and helpful as he can. The question, then, is not, What narrow category does it fit? but, How effective is the sermon? If it is effective, then the label does not matter.

But this consideration does raise another problem which must be considered. In the last chapter, and all through this one, has run the unanswered question, "Are all Christian sermons biblical?" What about sermons which do not fit the biblical category as defined? Are they Christian, if not biblical? We have given a definition of biblical preaching which makes imperative the preacher's serious study of specific scripture before him. Certainly no sermon can be considered biblical which does not require this intensive kind of biblical exegesis. Many would contend that all preaching must be exegetical-expository, and hence biblical.

Many Americans, at least, have trouble with such a

concept. Realizing a certain amount of defensiveness due to their lack of exegetical tools (i.e., original languages), they feel that every Christian sermon is not necessarily biblical. For example, some contend that sermons are either biblical (as defined) or topical; that is, the sermon either rises from the biblical passage or it rises from a Christian topic. Consider a doctrinal sermon. A preacher might set before himself a series of doctrinal sermons on the Apostle's Creed. "I Believe in God the Father Almighty" as the first statement in the creed might be the first sermon in the series. Chances are, the treatment of this creedal statement will be topical, theologically treated in a systematic way. If it is biblical, it will be so only in the ultimate sense that all theology is based finally on biblical ideas. But the specific treatment of this material will no doubt come from theological categories on the nature of God. Such a sermon would undoubtedly be Christian but not necessarily biblical.

Also, it is possible that a topic of tremendous social concern cries to be treated in the pulpit. Most American pulpits feel constrained to treat certain issues which do not necessarily grow out of the preacher's day-by-day scriptural study, whether he uses a lexicon or not. If he chooses to address himself to the problem of alcohol, he knows that biblical grounds alone will not help him too much. (The Bible can be used against his case.) Does this mean he cannot address himself to the subject? Granted that a lot of "sermons" are not sermons and a lot of subjects are not worthy of the pulpit, it does seem unusually narrow to rule out any discourses save those which can clearly be shown to be exegetical.

In summary, it is perhaps too strong to declare that only exegetical sermons are worthy to be called sermons. Not all effective sermons fit this category, even though it might be well to introduce another term such as "discourse" or "homily" to describe the sermon that is not strictly biblical. What is being maintained here is that preachers need to know what a biblical sermon is and to preach it. Many so-called biblical sermons are not scriptural, for they make no attempt to understand seriously the specific scripture on which the sermon is based. Further, it is maintained that such biblical preaching should be the rule of our preaching, not the exception. Christian preaching is *primarily* biblical preaching. For only as we faithfully interpret the Bible can we be aware of God's Word to us, for that is where he speaks to his faithful. Then when we have heard his Word within the words of Scripture, we can bring it to his people through our words, knowing that he alone, through the Holy Spirit, is the authenticator of our preaching.

CHAPTER IV

Proclaiming the Word Through the Doctrines of the Church

Someone has said that ours is an age which hungers for affirmations. If this is true, then there is a challenge as well as a danger for the preacher. It is dangerous in that many people are waiting expectantly for some authoritarian to give them simple answers to complex problems. A pulpit charlatan can take advantage of the thirst for verities, and quench that thirst with dogmatism. It is no accident that in times such as ours, dogmatism flourishes—both inside the church and out. People are seeking something into which they can put their trust; preachers of one kind or another are anxious to provide authoritarian answers to uncritical questions.

On the other hand, this is a challenging time for the preacher of Christ's gospel. People are indeed hungry for affirmations—affirmations of the gospel. The great truths of the Christian faith will get a hearing and a response if they are proclaimed from the pulpit. The preacher who has been feeding his people on the fruits of topical preaching cannot answer these deep needs. Someone has described Matthew Arnold as a "mournful evangelist who somehow contrived to lose his gospel." This is no time for mournful evangelists who have no more gospel than that which is found in the morning newspaper. For if we believe the Christian gospel, then we know man's basic problem is a theological one. A pulpit which turns its attention to man's basic theological questions will not only fulfill its own function but will help people on the deepest levels.

Protestantism is often accused of vagueness in terms of belief, and rightly so. The churches are full of sincere people who utter a babel of sounds when it comes to basic Christian beliefs. The same could be said in a group of Christian ministers. We hear complaints on every hand about the lack of a theological base to Protestantism. We are alarmed at the lack of doctrinal understanding of our youth, the inarticulateness of our mature laymen, and the nontheological preaching of the pulpits.

Many Protestant chaplains in the services were chagrined to see the clear pronouncements of their Roman Catholic brethren on almost any subject, while they, with the possible exception of a Lutheran or an Episcopalian or a fundamentalist sect representative, were often tongue-tied in the face of great crises. Someone said that in the face of death the Catholic chaplain performed the rite of extreme unction, while the Protestant chaplain lit a cigarette for the dying man. Mixed marriages have focused the problem for the parents of a son or daughter marrying a Catholic partner. They have found themselves unable to cope with the doctrines which have a part of such a relationship, and along with the son or daughter have felt little support for their vague feelings of apprehension. Tragically, they often have found little aid from their own ministers on a doctrinal level. The Protestant churches have, in all too many instances, been unsure, groping, and vague because of their lack of articulated theological principles which are meaningful to clergy and laity alike.

Yet the hunger persists among the people for some grounding which is intellectually respectable and relevant to human needs. Not long ago, in talking to a layman from a church that was without a minister, I was surprised to hear him say, "What we need here is not a minister but a Sunday-school teacher. We don't even know enough of the Christian faith to know whether to accept it or reject it." This indictment of the preaching office explains the feelings of many of our laymen. Certainly they are hungry theologically. At one time it was not fashionable to be interested in religion. Now it is. Even discounting the shallowness of much of the surge of religion, there is still a concern on the part of people to know about the faith.

Preachers are constantly shocked to hear laymen at parties bring up the names of Paul Tillich or Reinhold Niebuhr and show an acquaintance with their work. It is not unusual to hear a theological discussion or at least theological questions asked at cocktail parties. Our age and our climate are filled with theology, even though in many instances the expressions are naïve and outside the church. Any chaplain could attest to the theological questionings of the men in the armed services. The works of C. S. Lewis, Dorothy Sayers, and other such writers attest to the popularity of theology for the layman.

A few years ago, one minister sent out a questionnaire to his people, asking them to choose subjects in which they were interested. Out of the six topics chosen for sermon subjects, five of them were definitely doctrinal. Many preachers could offer similar testimonies out of their own experiences.

Why, then, in the face of the lack of doctrine and the desire for it, have we got into such a state? Why is there such a soft voice coming from the pulpit in terms of doctrinal utterances?

It would undoubtedly take an expert in the field of American church history to trace the absence of doctrine in the churches. There are, however, some reasons which must be apparent to all.

For one thing, many denominations pride themselves on being *undoctrinal* or *untheological.* "Theology" and "doctrine" are sinister words, and represent an unwanted authoritarianism or dogmatism usually associated with the Roman Catholic Church. Therefore, doctrine is associated with dogma and rejected as being rigid, cold, abstract, and irrelevant. This criticism is directed, not only at the Roman church, but toward many of the Reformation churches as well, particularly an alleged Calvinism.

Close to this, of course, is the American's concern with experience as derived from the nineteenth-century revivalistic movement. Theology was not crucial on the frontier. Theological problems were left on the Continent. What was important was new behavior; hence, revivalism emphasized pietism and experience as tests of a new Christian life. The Christian-experience motif has always been strong in the Protestant evangelical denominations, with a corresponding lack of interest in theology. This condition still persists. "It is not what you believe, but how you act that counts" can still be heard in pews, and in the pulpit as well.

We are also a pragmatic nation. This is not only true of religion, but equally true in literature, philosophy, and education. We are practical men, and theological thinking is abstract and often impractical. If religion "helps" us, then let it do so without worrying too much about what it all means. Such an attitude is prevalent in American churches.

Along with all this is the thought in America that the churches are pretty much culture reflectors. This is what Will Herberg is affirming in *Catholic, Protestant, and Jew*. Our major faiths are three facets of the same thing—an American faith which is bound up with our heritage and related to the American way without much specific content. If this is true, then it is easy to see why theology is not too important.

Similarly, we live in a mobile age as far as churches are concerned generally. Our population is uprooted constantly. It is not unusual for comity programs in a new housing development to throw Baptists, Methodists, and Presbyterians into one community church. In such irenic situations doctrinal differences are minimized. Even where the local church is not a community church, any denominational church in a newer area may be filled with a host of other denominations. With a concern for growing memberships and growing churches, emphasis upon doctrine can be avoided. It is not unheard of to see a Baptist church taking, on transfer, members who have never been immersed. A Methodist from the Midwest transferred to New England may enter a Congregational church without much discernible difference. A Presbyterian from the East may feel very much at home in a community church in Southern California. Even the ecumenical movement has had its effect. The desire to come together has, in many instances, blurred the differences and made us feel guilty about doctrines that would keep us from fellowship with others. Hence, there has been a conscious effort to play down those things which keep us apart.

During the war a chaplain was accosted by a Merchant Marine lieutenant who had been drinking. When he saw the cross on the chaplain's sleeve, he pulled his chair over to the table and began to pour out a tale of woe. Psychologists tell us that there is a stage of inebriation which brings out religiosity, and this lieutenant was at that stage. He told of his many sins, but assured the chaplain that he was reared in a strict Presbyterian home. He admitted that he had departed from that faith and had particularly been interested in the Far-Eastern religions discovered in his travels. Finally, he said, "I guess you would say that I'm a Presbyterian with Buddhist leanings." How many ministers could say that they have members with Buddhist leanings? This story may be a parable of our time.

Nevertheless, there is the haunting question that if we are ignorant of theology, then how can we be Christian? Since theology is talk about God, then is it not basic to our faith? Is it not possible that some of our paucity of vitality in the Protestant church is the result of our lack of doctrinal preaching to give an understanding to our faith?

But to those of us who have avoided doctrinal preaching, it can be a forbidding experience to both pulpit and pew. Even though people are hungry to hear about the faith, they have reservations about a dogmatic confrontation. C. S. Lewis puts it graphically in a story about an old R.A.F. officer who confronted him when he began a talk on theology:

> I've no use for all that stuff. But, mind you, I'm a religious man too. I *know* there's a God. I've *felt* Him: out alone in the desert at night: the tremendous mystery. And that's just why I don't believe all your neat little dogmas and formulas about Him. To anyone who's met the real thing they all seem so petty and pedantic and unreal! [1]

How many ministers have heard some such expression from one of their laymen? Indeed, how many ministers themselves have either voiced or felt some similar sentiment? But now see Lewis' answer to this criticism of theology:

> Now in a sense I quite agreed with that man. I think he'd probably had a real experience of God in the desert. And when he turned from that experience to the Christian creeds, I think he *was* really turning from something quite real to something less real. In the same way, if a man has once looked at the Atlantic from the beach, and then goes and looks at a map of the Atlantic, he also will be turning from something more real to something less real: turning from real waves to a bit of coloured paper. But here comes the point.

[1] *Beyond Personality* (New York: The Macmillan Company, 1945), p. 1. Used by permission of the publishers, The Macmillan Company and Geoffrey Bles Ltd.

The map *is* only coloured paper, but there are two things you have to remember about it. In the first place, it is based on what hundreds and thousands of people have found out by sailing the real Atlantic. In that way it has behind it masses of experience just as real as the one you could have from the beach; only, while yours would be a single isolated glimpse, the map fits all those different experiences together. In the second place, if you want to go anywhere, the map is absolutely necessary. As long as you're content with walks on the beach, your own glimpses are far more fun than looking at a map. But the map's going to be more use than walks on the beach if you want to get to America.

Well, Theology's like the map.[2]

Even though Christians may be hungry for affirmations, paradoxically they are often nervous about theology. Yet, as Lewis says, if they want to get anywhere in their faith, then theology is absolutely necessary.

Even those who purport to be anti- or nontheological are in reality reacting against a *kind* of theology rather than against theology itself. All of us, whether we want to be or not, are theologians. This title does not come with ordination, but is the name given to anyone who talks about God, whether systematically or not. Henry Sloane Coffin writes that "doctrines are man's attempts, always provisional, to rationalize his experiences of God." [3] If Anselm is right that theology is "faith seeking understanding" then no Christian preacher can really disclaim theology.

[2] *Ibid.*, pp. 1-2.

[3] Henry Sloane Coffin, *What to Preach* (New York: George H. Doran Co., 1926), p. 48.

He may, however, react negatively to certain kinds of theology, or he may disclaim interest in dogma or creeds. For this reason, doctrinal preaching should be seen in at least three forms. First, when one speaks of doctrinal preaching he usually means in the formal, accepted statements of the historical church; that is, a preacher may preach a series of sermons based on the Apostles' Creed, the Nicene Creed, the Westminster Confession, the Articles of Religion, etc. Such sermons would attempt to set forth the doctrine as formulated in some such historical statement which embodies the essentials of the Christian faith. To some this is what preaching doctrine means—and all that it means. To others, this is too narrow, limiting doctrine to only those churches who ascribe their faith in creedal statements, or limiting doctrine to systematic treatment.

For these reasons, it appears that a second way to handle doctrine is to think of doctrinal preaching more broadly. Those who disclaim creedal statements as the basis of faith nonetheless preach doctrines. All preachers preach a doctrine of God, Person and Work of Christ, the efficacy of the Atonement, and other classical doctrines. They may not do so systematically, but they do so nevertheless. A Baptist will not preach from the Apostles' Creed, perhaps, but he undoubtedly will preach on the doctrine of baptism. If Coffin's definition is correct, then most Christian preaching will have doctrine in it whether it is typed as that or not.

Doctrine enters preaching in still another way. Doctrine thought of in the broadest sense permeates all Christian preaching, reaching into every aspect of faith and life.

The Christian life and its duties, while ordinarily thought of as, say, "life-situation," are in reality in the realm of personal and social ethics which evolve from doctrine. That is, ethics and doctrine are inseparable. When we preach ethics we are also preaching doctrine, if only by implication.

The preacher must not only consider the way in which he treats doctrine, specifically or incidentally; he must also consider the aim and purpose of the doctrinal sermon. What is he attempting to do in the sermon? Here again there are at least two aims, purposes, or forms the sermon may take.

First, doctrinal preaching is often considered evangelistic. Or perhaps we could say evangelistic preaching is doctrinal. Historically, this is undoubtedly true. The preacher holds up man's sin and God's grace, calls for repentance and faith. Even such a simplification of the evangelist's essential message demonstrates that he is engaged primarily in proclaiming the doctrines of the church.

Second, it is also possible to think of doctrinal preaching in terms of education. This preaching is basically *didache*. After the Christian has responded in faith, he needs to be fed and nurtured. This is the task of all faithful pastors; so he may find himself spending many sermons in his pastorate in interpreting the beliefs of the church in order that his people may become knowledgeable in their experience, more articulate in witnessing to it, and more earnest in their churchmanship.

While both these purposes are admirable, they may tend to compartmentalize doctrinal preaching into set types. In the first instance, doctrinal preaching may be limited to certain seasons as well as to a certain approach. Too, the approach itself may be limiting. Since an important aspect of evangelistic preaching is to motivate the will, there is neither time nor inclination to unfold meaningfully the underlying doctrines of the gospel. The approach, necessarily emotional, may leave the preacher simply articulating the words, phrases, or jargon of the gospel without treating the meanings. This is not to say that effective evangelism is devoid of thought; it *is* to say that the approach is primarily emotional, not rational.

The second use of doctrine as teaching also has limitations. The danger here is that the preacher will neglect the kerygma, the evangel, the proclamation. He will be explaining the meaning of the doctrine and may not proclaim anew the good news which should be part of every sermon. In other words, he may give a lecture on systematic theology. Although this in itself would have merit in an adult study program, in the pulpit it violates the nature of a sermon, neglects the kerygmatic proclamation, and avoids the call to commitment and response which is the motivational concern of all preaching.

In reality what we are saying is that a doctrinal sermon (or doctrinal preaching) as usually thought of may be suspect in itself. This is not to say that doctrine is not to be preached. We have seen the urgent necessity for the preacher to unfold the doctrines of the church in his preaching. What is crucial is how this material is handled. A so-called doctrinal sermon, while necessarily handling much important theological material, may also demonstrate many of the weaknesses of doctrinal preaching by setting out to preach doctrine for its own sake.

What is at stake is the purpose of preaching. Should it ever be to preach doctrine, to preach Bible, to preach social concerns? Is not the concern of the pulpit to proclaim the kerygma in its fullest—here and now? If so, then this must be the purpose of our preaching.

But the way the proclamation is unfolded is another matter, and the crux of the problem for handling doctrinal materials. The proclamation, of course, is itself doctrinal. This means that any faithful preaching of the gospel is doctrinal preaching in the broadest and best sense. What we are saying, then, is that a doctrinal sermon as a type is highly suspect, but preaching doctrinally is mandatory.

The preacher's task becomes, then, not one of category or type, but of how he may handle doctrinal material within a given sermon. With this in mind, no matter what the preacher's individual sermon form may take, we can look at some considerations for handling theological materials in the pulpit.

The first word is that the doctrinal material should be *relevant,* with all that that hackneyed word can connote. We have said earlier that the Christian gospel is incarnational—God was in Christ, then and *now,* reconciling the world to himself. At no place does this become more important in preaching than in handling doctrinal concepts. Someone once suggested that the preacher gets hold of doctrine at its preaching end. True! In fact, one might argue that doctrine which cannot be preached effectively to the man in the pew is not essential doctrine after all.

The relevancy of doctrinal preaching can easily be seen, negatively. Many sermons fail at this point, remaining abstract and full of jargon, and sound considerably like a lecture in systematic theology. For example, a preacher may be considering such a subject as the Person of Jesus Christ. It is probable that there will be at least two correct, Christian affirmations made: Jesus was divine; Jesus was human. Many of these sermons stop there. So what? is a good response to such a sermon. It may be enlightening, helpful to our understanding of Christology, and well presented. But is it a sermon? Where is the call to commitment? What makes the divine-human nature relevant to the bus driver? Where is the motivation to commit oneself to the Master? This abstract manner of handling theology has just about killed doctrinal preaching, and adds to the uninitiated's criticism of doctrine as being simply rational and irrelevant.

To achieve relevance, the preacher should be concrete and avoid abstractions. This is easier to state than achieve, for we do deal with abstractions in religion. Nevertheless, the preacher's lifelong task is to make concepts such as "God," "love," "salvation," concrete in the experience of those who sit before him. Although the task is never ending, the preacher each week faces the same problem of making the concepts of theology and faith intersect the experiences of those who sit in the pew.

To do this he must first of all come to terms with his language. Language is the medium through which he transmits his ideas. He must be sure that his language is a fit vehicle to carry its theological load. He should avoid jargon. It is amazing how much of a preacher's workaday world is carried on through a language which might be characterized as *theologese*. In seminary halls and ministerial meetings such jargon has the advantage of being a shorthand way of getting the day-by-day work done. The same would undoubtedly be true for doctors, accountants, and baseball players. In the pulpit, however, the preacher's language may be the means of keeping the revealed God hidden. Such terms as the "atoning blood of Jesus," "the covenanted community," "existential," "demythologizing," should be kept in the classroom or the study, not in the pulpit.

But the use of language is deeper than that of jargon. Actually, language is deeper than words themselves; it is concerned with meanings. That is why the plaintive cry to change the vocabulary of Christianity to a twentieth-century vocabulary remains largely a plaintive cry. For while jargon is to be avoided, there is a great deal of difference between using specialized words and using traditional religious language in a meaningful way. Many of those who desire to change religious terminology really wish to get rid of the concept. It may be we do not like the word "sin" because we do not like the concept "sin"; therefore, if we can get rid of the word we can get rid of the concept. What other word could we possibly use for "sin" as it is understood in the Christian tradition? Or "grace"? On the deepest level, then, the preacher needs to come to an understanding himself of these hallowed Christian words, and then to use them meaningfully and in a context which will make them "come alive" to his listeners.

The basis of the preacher's handling of doctrine on the level of relevance finally comes down to how real he can make his material to those who sit in front of him. This is the acid test of preaching doctrinally. How helpful, clear, and relevant is it to the average man in the pew? In the example used earlier, concerning the sermon on the Person of Jesus Christ, it was suggested that the two major points would be:

I. JESUS WAS DIVINE
II. JESUS WAS HUMAN

Such a sermon would probably be abstract, intellectual, and devoid of relevance. Suppose the preacher added:

III. JESUS IS SAVIOR

Such a point would force him to look at the Master in terms of what he does for those who preach sermons and sit in pews. It is not being suggested that point three of every sermon is tagged on in order to drag into the sermon a relevant note on which to end. Indeed, all the points should be relevant in the best sense of that word. It is important, however, that a sermon have a call for commitment. This call necessitates a lively encounter between the gospel and the people in order that they might respond. In this sense the last point does focus the importance of relevance in the sermon. This particular sermon, if it avoided the jargon which plagues many sermons on salvation, could be a meaningful interpretation of how God affects our lives through Christ in a specific and concrete way. It might be a good practice for each preacher to have a specific person in his mind's eye as he prepares his sermon. "Here is Mrs. Jones, housewife. How will this be meaningful to her?" "There sits Dr. Williams. How does this become clear to him?" "There is Bill Howard, carpenter. What will this say to him?"

Occasionally it is heard that the preacher should not be

concerned with relevance. The gospel is self-authenticating; the preacher may abuse or pare down the Word in order to make it simple and concrete. Of course, it is true that the gospel cannot be packaged like aspirin tablets in an easy-to-take form. The transcendent God defies our inclinations to encompass him in our understanding. The numinous concept of God forbids a free and easy glibness about him. Indeed, the *mysterium tremendum* defies all our theologizing. Yet, when this has been said, it is nevertheless true that as God's spokesmen we are attempting to make his will and his ways known to men. Granting our failures of tongue and idea, we should not permit his infiniteness to be our rationalization for abstract and irrelevant discourse.

To attempt the concreteness of theology, we are brought to the importance of analogy. We need to be honest at the outset, and admit that analogy is weak as a proof of anything. It is illustrative at best. We know that we cannot really compare the known with the unknown, the animate with the inanimate, or the finite with the infinite. Yet, analogical language is about the only way we can talk about God. So, if we don't ask it to do more for us than it can, an analogy may be the most meaningful way of treating religious truth.

An example of this relevant use of analogy to make clear a theological concept can be found in many places. Here is a modern parable by Theodore O. Wedel, which he used to underscore the danger of self-worship in the life of our churches—a self-worship which neglects the church's mission.

Picture a coastguard or life-saving station on a dangerous coast. It has stood for centuries, and tales of its rescue service are treasured by the successors to the founders. In the course of time, indeed, those who manned the rescue service turned to expanding and beautifying the station itself. Do not "life-savers" deserve comfort and a rest home to fit them for their arduous task? Architects vied with one another in building for them a dwelling place worthy of their vocation. Honorary though not active members joined in lending support. Nor was the rescue station designed merely for those whose duty it was to launch the life-boats. The rescued in their turn deserved warm beds and proper food.

This station-building, however, became in time an absorbing activity that rescue service itself was increasingly neglected, although traditional rescue drills and rituals were carefully preserved. The actual launching out into ocean storms became a hireling vocation or one left to a few volunteers. What was even more a deflection of the original charter of the station, when the dedicated volunteers brought in their boatloads of the shipwrecked—men of alien color and speech, maimed and encrusted with ocean slime—the custodians of the rescue station were disconcerted and disturbed. "Will they not," so they were tempted to exclaim, "soil the linen in our clean beds, and, moved by gratitude for salvation, desire to become life savers themselves and thus presume to belong by right to our intimate fellowship? Should we not set up a minimum entrance requirement of cleanliness and good manners before we offer shelter? We can, at least, urge them to build a life-saving station of their own at a decorous distance from our own." [4]

[4] "Evangelism—The Mission of the Church to Those Outside Her Life," *The Ecumenical Review,* October, 1953, p. 24.

Or, here's an analogy of how God works in history.

When we think of the action of God in history—and present it to ourselves in pictures, as we are almost bound to do—we need not imagine a heavy hand interposed to interfere with the working of a heavy piece of machinery. Perhaps a better picture of our situation would be that of a child who played her piece very badly when she was alone, but when the music-teacher sat at her side played it passably well, though the music-teacher never touched her, never said anything, but operated by pure sympathetic attraction and by just being there.[5]

A final one concluded a sermon on the nature of God's forgiving love.

Suppose you knew a family where there had been unfaithfulness on the part of the husband. The family was torn asunder, the husband left, and the wife was broken-hearted. But suppose he repents and desires to restore the relationship. Actually, there is nothing he can do to effect this renewal. A mink coat, flowers, candy, a Cadillac, or diamond necklace will not buy his way back into his family's affection. For the heart of for*give*ness is the word *give* and only the wife out of the agony of her suffering can restore that relationship by forgiving the errant husband. But suppose she does forgive and the family is restored; not forgiving and remembering when things go wrong, but forgiving and loving even more deeply than before. It is difficult for us to envision this kind

[5] H. Butterfield, *Christianity and History* (New York: Charles Scribner's Sons, 1950), p. 111.

of love in a human situation. How much more difficult to see the love of God manifested on a cross.[6]

Such an illustration does not exhaust the nature of God's love, but it does say something about what it is like on a level most of us can understand.

If the first word about preaching doctrine concerns *relevance* with concern for language, meanings, and analogy, the second major word to be said about doctrinal preaching is that it should be *biblical.* We have attempted to define biblical preaching as proclaiming the gospel of good news through specific biblical materials in a relevant way. While we have not said that all preaching should be biblical, we have come close to that affirmation. In the main, the definition should hold for doctrinal preaching. A specific biblical grounding will help to escape the systematic-theology lecture in the pulpit. To escape the temptation to be too glib about the Infinite, the biblical setting will do what those writers did—tell of the faith they had in God's mighty works, not try to explain in a rational way his existence and attributes. A sermon on reconciliation apart from the Bible will be the language and thought of the law court, but not necessarily biblical or Christian. Love apart from the Bible loses the motif of vicarious suffering. Sin discussed away from a biblical grounding may become cosmic guilt, eliminating the personal thrust of sin found in the Bible.

[6] An unpublished sermon by the author. The idea was suggested originally by Theodore O. Wedel's discussion of "Theology by Analogy." See *Pulpit Rediscovers Theology* (Greenwich, Conn.: The Seabury Press, 1956), pp. 100 ff.

Of course, it is true that a preacher may preach on the doctrines embodied in the creed or some other Christian doctrine apart from specific biblical foundations. He may assert that all doctrines are, in the final sense, biblical. In this way he will set forth to preach a sermon, say on the doctrine of creation, apart from specific text or setting. Certainly there is room for this kind of instruction. But this direct approach to doctrine is so fraught with peril that the preacher should be wary and ought not be surprised if it becomes lecturish, abstract, or intellectual.

The proclamation of the good news is itself a doctrinal task, and in this sense every sermon is a doctrinal one. But the good news is found within the Bible where God's Word becomes ours as he speaks through its words to us. Thus, in finding his sources there, the preacher will commit himself to preaching week by week from the Bible. He will cover doctrines of the church out of the biblical-theological setting which reflects the personal and existential nature of theology. Here we can see how it is difficult to talk about doctrinal sermons as a type. Is not the preacher really preaching only one sermon? His characteristic sermon should be one which is biblically based and doctrinally sound. This kind of preaching should make less necessary the preacher's preoccupation with a Lenten series on doctrine; he is doing it week by week by preaching faithfully the Word of God.

CHAPTER V

Proclaiming the Word to People: Life Situations

One of the most popular forms of American preaching is what has been called "life-situation" preaching. For want of a better definition, such preaching may be regarded as that which deals with people's problems. It is considered to be person-centered, getting its start from some situation in life which the congregation faces, and then bringing the gospel to bear upon it. These problems are usually personal, centering upon some internal concern such as misfortune, feelings of guilt, family tensions, etc. It has the advantage and relevance of beginning where people are and then dealing with that problem in light of Christian resources.

An excellent example of such preaching is found in the analysis furnished by Harold W. Ruopp.[1] From 1931 to 1938, Ruopp secured answers from 6,356 persons

[1] "Life Situation Preaching," *The Christian Century Pulpit,* XII, 5 and 6 (May and June, 1941).

to the question: "What is the outstanding question (problem or difficulty) which you face in your thinking and living?" He arranged the answers in a syllabus around the following categories: the individual and his inner self; the individual and his relationship to the family; the individual and his relationship to larger social groups and society; and the individual in his relationship to God and the universe. Almost 50 per cent of the responses are placed in the first group, dealing with such concerns as personality problems and difficulties; life decisions; moral problems; educational needs; misfortune; thwarted ambitions and desires; the meaning of life; indifference to religious living; personal feelings of sin and guilt. These responses, plus those in the other categories, reveal the kinds of personal concerns which Ruopp collected from his questionnaire. As he says, "This study, with all its shortcomings, does give us a fairly adequate picture of the major life situations with which every preacher must deal, and for which he must meticulously prepare himself." [2] Presumably, life-situation preaching is that which takes one of these issues close to the congregation and deals with it in a Christian context. Ruopp suggests that a pattern for such a sermon could be:

I. WE ARE HERE
II. HOW DID WE GET HERE?
III. HOW DO WE GET OUT OF HERE?

Recognizing the temptation to deal more with the problem than with the solution, he suggests that the major portion of the sermon be concerned with point III.

[2] *Ibid.*, XII, 6, p. 141.

Another well-known "life-situation" preacher of the same period is James Gordon Gilkey. Such a book of sermons as *When Life Gets Hard* [3] demonstrates his method of dealing with the problems faced by his congregation. Most of the sermons begin with a problem which is identified and described; or a case study; or a literary example; or even a biblical example. In each instance the take-off is at some point which connects with a real concern of the congregation. After such a problem is established, the rest of the sermon is devoted to what can be done about it. A typical outline might look like this:

I. PROBLEM
II.
III.
IV.
V.

II, III, IV, and V deal with the question: What can be done about it? One such sermon is entitled "When You Have Too Much to Do." It begins with Sinclair Lewis' novel *Babbitt,* which describes a hustling businessman anxiously pushing to get ahead and making sure that everyone in his office is hustling too. From this, Gilkey suggests that we too are concerned with managing an impossible array of jobs and an overlong succession of working hours. He asks if the problem can be solved. Can we survive when we have far too much to do? He affirms that the problem can be solved if we gain inward quietness. How can we acquire this serenity? First, talk to yourself about your own hidden powers (reserves of strength).

[3] (New York: The Macmillan Company, 1945).

Second, talk to yourself about the busy day you are facing. Remind yourself that the day will probably bring nothing more than a long succession of *little* tasks, not big battles. Also, no matter how crowded the day, you will not have to work continuously. Third, you should remind yourself of the technique of working effectively. Close the mind to anxieties, stop regretting, and quit entertaining fears. Concentrate all attention on the single task at hand. This is gained through self-discipline.[4]

The best philosophical statement of this type of preaching was made by Harry Emerson Fosdick in an article in *Harper's Magazine* in July, 1928. The article, entitled "What Is the Matter with Preaching," set forth the platform upon which life-situation preaching rests:

> Every sermon should have for its main business the solving of some problem—a vital, important problem, puzzling minds, burdening consciences, distracting lives—and any sermon which thus does tackle a real problem, throw even a little light on it, and help some individuals practically to find their way through it cannot be altogether uninteresting.[5]

Further, "this endeavor to help people to solve their spiritual problems is a sermon's only justifiable aim." [6] It is obvious that Fosdick was revolting against a sterile kind of biblical preaching which was largely irrelevant to the twentieth-century mind. Without at this point going into all that was involved in this revolt from a wooden, expository method of preaching, it is clear that Fosdick is here

[4] *Ibid.*, pp. 35-46.
[5] July, 1928, p. 134.
[6] *Ibid.*, p. 134.

reversing both the concern and the starting point of a sermon. He says in another place in this article, "The modern preacher . . . should start with that [human living], should clearly visualize some real need, perplexity, sin, or desire in his auditors, and then should throw on the problem all the light he can find in the Scripture or anywhere else." [7] It is clear that to Fosdick the starting point of a sermon is not necessarily some biblical text, nor is the content to be necessarily an exposition of scripture. Rather, it is to begin with a human need and then solve the problem arising in that need.

It should be pointed out that many of his followers did not take seriously his entire article. He also says in this article that topical preachers should not depart from the Bible and use their own ideas. Neither should they turn their pulpits into platforms, nor their sermons into lectures. But it is clear that he was calling for a different approach in preaching. He suggested that the pulpit should emulate the project method of teaching, where as pedagogy begins, not with the subject, but with the child. He levels strictures against dogmatic preaching and pleas for cooperative thinking between the preacher and his congregation. In short, "Preaching is wrestling with individuals over questions of life and death, and until that idea of it commands a preacher's mind and method, eloquence will avail him little and theology not at all." [8]

There are more recent statements of the importance and method of life-situation preaching, but they are all similar to Fosdick's in their emphasis. Halford E. Luccock de-

[7] *Ibid.*, p. 135.
[8] *Ibid.*, p. 141.

votes considerable time to this method of approach.[9] He suggests that the preacher should begin where people are, and even uses as an example John Dewey's pattern of reflective thinking as a possible approach for the life-situation preacher:

1. A felt difficulty
2. Location and definition of the difficulty
3. Suggestion of possible solutions
4. Development by reasoning of bearings of suggestions
5. Further observation and exploration leading to acceptance or rejection of the solution.[10]

In Luccock's analysis, life-situation preaching has many advantages, some of which are: saving one from vague generalities; saving one from preaching the same sermon every Sunday; and keeping preachers from moving from their basic material—people. In particular, he emphasizes the importance of people as a source of sermons and advises the preacher to be therefore concerned with them.

It is clear from all the foregoing examples that life-situation preaching is an endeavor to be practical, relevant, and helpful. But to view it accurately one must see it in its historical perspective. Without endeavoring to give a full-blown treatment to the history of contemporary preaching, it is helpful to see this development in American preaching against the backdrop of what went before.

[9] *Op. cit.,* chs. 6, 7, and 8.
[10] *Ibid.,* p. 56.

The changes that occurred in this century affecting science, philosophy, and theology in time affected the pulpits. This revolution was in part the growth of the scientific method brought on by Darwin; the corresponding rise of the scientific method of Bible study; the rise of urbanization and industrialization with the church's response in terms of the social gospel. These factors, along with World War I and the great depression, all conspired to change preaching patterns in a vast section of Protestant pulpits. Add to this the struggle against fundamentalism and the new psychological studies of man, and one begins to see how a new approach to preaching took place in the major denominations of this country.

This new approach—which gets its philosophic statement from Fosdick—is in a real sense, then, a product of our own cultural and religious heritage. It is uniquely American and is one of the major causes for the European criticism of the American pulpit as being too practical, too conscious of being up to date, too nonbiblical, too nontheological, and too man-centered.

But before we examine the basis of this criticism, we must look again at what this new movement in preaching was aiming to do. It was indeed revolting against a kind of sterile biblical exegesis which was the basis for preaching at an earlier time. Fosdick also suggests in this same article that the modern congregation could not care less what happened to the Jebusites. The newer emphasis was in a sense anti- or perhaps nonbiblical. The same way with theology. The modern preacher, revolting against the fundamentalism of his father, was concerned to make the gospel meaningful to modern man on his terms. Thus, the concern for people and their problems; a concern for relevant and meaningful language; a concern for communication; and above all a concern for issues and ideas that were of importance to those who sat in the pews each Sunday. It is not difficult to see that to some this movement was a shift from God's Word to man's word—a shift from God-centeredness to man-centeredness.

Although the life-situation type of sermon is still standard fare in hosts of pulpits all across America, there has been a considerable reaction against such preaching. The earlier chapters in this book are predicated, in part, on such a reaction. The resurgence of biblical-theological interests, commonly called crisis theology, caused a revolution in many pulpits, and the life-situation approach was one of the victims. Actually, though, no one factor has been involved. World War II put a damper on the easy optimism of many pulpits afflicted with life-situation sermons as the only diet. The whole reawakening of biblical and theological studies has caused a re-evaluation of the emphasis of our pulpits. If this revolution was triggered by the continental neo-Reformation emphasis, it nevertheless found friends who were not of that theological persuasion. For even those who were purportedly devotees of life-situation preaching warned of its dangers. We have already suggested that Fosdick was wary of turning the pulpit into a platform or making sermons into lectures. And Halford Luccock, who emphasized the importance of such preaching, was well aware of the dangers that accrued to such a method. He warned that life-situation preaching could cause a lack of variety in preaching. He went on to affirm that such preaching could be very wooden, dealing constantly with stock situations. One of his greatest strictures was that such preaching might fail to confront people with God because it was so concerned with human problems. Further, he felt that much of so-called life-situation preaching substituted psychology for religion. Finally, such a preacher became so "practical" that he became didactic.[11]

With this important background in mind, it is now time to look specifically at the concerns of this chapter. What does it mean to proclaim the Word to people? Is life-situation preaching a valid way of doing so? In what way, if any, does person-centered preaching contradict what we have said earlier concerning biblical preaching as the norm for the pulpit? Is biblical-doctrinal preaching incompatible with life-situation preaching?

The first word to be said about life-situation preaching in regard to proclaiming the Word is that so-called life-situation preaching is probably not a type in itself. Earlier it was suggested that, although biblical preaching should be our norm, it was held to be conceivable that there could be Christian preaching without its being biblical. If so, and this *if* is highly debatable, there are only two major types of sermons. The other major type, apart from biblical, would be *topical*. To make the distinction clear, a biblical sermon is one which develops from a scriptural base or insight; a topical sermon develops from a topic of the preacher's choosing, usually current. To put it another way, the preacher stands in two worlds: one world is the gospel and all that it connotes, including the Bible; the

[11] *Ibid.*, pp. 85-92.

other foot stands in the present-day world—a world of *topics.* These topics which result in sermons may be biographical (Kagawa); socioethical (temperance); problem solving (school integration); occasional (baccalaureate); doctrinal (as we saw earlier, doctrinal preaching as often practiced may be considered topical when it begins with a topic such as "the nature of God" without a biblical base); or life-situation (personal problem). American preaching, presumably, gets started at either point. This distinction between topical and biblical is helpful—if not desirable—for it describes the pulpit practice of American preachers. As to life-situation preaching, it makes clear where it belongs and points to the dangers which it and the other examples of topical preaching have: a departure from biblical rootage and a corresponding diminution of the kerygmatic proclamation.

Granting the merits of such a criticism of topical preaching, there is much to be said for its claims. We have seen that such preaching (and here we speak of topical, for in reality it subsumes life-situation as a type) was a revolt against an earlier sterile and wooden method of handling biblical materials. We have seen how topical preaching attempted to deal honestly and realistically with personal problems that people faced rather than assuming they would be thirsting to hear about some genealogy in Numbers. This approach tended to deal with specific problems, and this was especially significant as the church tried to deal realistically with the many social concerns confronting it. Further, it took seriously the congregation which sat before the preacher. It rejected any idea that the gospel needed neither interpretation nor receivers to make it effective. Above all it was concerned with people and the efforts needed to communicate with them effectively.

If these reasons do not justify the existence of topical preaching, they do explain why it came about. If this is an American phenomenon, then it should not be despised for being that; it should be understood. Just as a postwar, disillusioned Europe spawned neo-orthodoxy after World War I, so a narrow, sterile biblicism created the topical preacher in America. No matter that each reaction becomes extreme and the pendulum swings wider than it should; the topical preacher's manifesto as exemplified in Fosdick's article was an expected, if not completely desirable, reaction. The biblical-theological renaissance through which we have now been passing has reacted (the pendulum again) against such topical preaching; and, as can be expected, this reaction has been extreme in some quarters.

The major criticism against topical preaching has already been implied. There is the danger that the gospel is left out. The problems developed are often "solved" on the human level through psychology, sociology, or other disciplines apart from the Christian gospel. Apart from raising the purpose of preaching (chapter I), this approach often fails to confront people with God, and keeps both the problem and solution on the human plane. The first problem the topical preacher has to face is to find a Christian topic. He must ask himself if the topic he has selected is really Christian. Does it grow out of the Christian faith, and does the Christian faith have something to say to what he is considering? Such actual topics as "Moses Was a Methodist," "Facing the New Year Without George Bernard Shaw," and "Overcoming Fatigue" are examples of subjects which are not suitable for the pulpit because they are not Christian topics.

Another problem the topical preacher faces is his use of the Bible in topical sermons, including, of course, life-situation as well as the other types. It should be clear by this time *what* and *how important* biblical preaching is. We shall come back to it again, but at this point it is enough to say that most topical sermons *use* the Bible rather than letting the Bible use them. A topical sermon—in search of a text and biblical support, if indeed it uses the Bible at all—will tend to select biblical materials at random as it would any other source to support its points. As we have already seen, this procedure cannot be called biblical preaching.

Another problem with topical preaching is that much of it is not significant. Perhaps this is another way of indicating that it is difficult to find Christian topics. We have pointed out three sermon topics which are dubious as Christian topics. They could receive the same indictment as to their significance. Many topical pulpits, in their endeavor to be fresh and interesting, cast far afield in selecting material for their sermons. This frantic anxiety to be up to date and relevant often turns the pulpit toward book reviewing, instruction in citizenship, and physical fitness, to name only three examples. Now of course from some perspectives any of these might be considered significant; however, the question for the preacher is, how significant are they for the pulpit?

Although it should be clear from the earlier chapters on the role of the preacher and the nature of preaching (biblical), that such topical preaching is highly suspect, as of now we can say that, if a preacher is devoted to topical preaching, the burden of proof is on him to *make* it Christian. He must ask himself, "Is this a Christian topic?" "Can this sermon be rooted in the Christian faith?" And above all, "Is this topic really significant?" If he can answer all these questions in the affirmative, then he may go on with his sermon. Even then he will be under a handicap if it is true, as this book suggests, that the normal sermon should be biblically based.

The basic problem with topical preaching (and therefore life-situation preaching as well) is that there is often a basic confusion between *content* and *form*. The life-situation (or topical) preacher is most often led astray when he thinks of such a sermon as having a specific content. That is, he may take a subject such as personal suffering, state the problem, analyze the reasons for suffering, suggest the reasons for suffering, and then give some advice for living with or overcoming suffering. He may even—and presumably would—use biblical materials and Christian affirmations along the way, but his approach is often intellectual, analytical; indeed, it may be primarily psychological. Such a treatment may be very helpful, but in the final analysis it is good advice, not good news. It runs the gravest risk—as all topical sermons do—of not getting the material off the human plane, of not proclaiming the good news of the gospel. Such preaching is more common than it ought to be in pulpits, and merits the charge that American preaching is nontheological, nonbiblical. When the preacher considers topics, situations, and problems, and builds his sermons in light of these subjects, then he will inevitably fall prey to such charges, especially if he feels that such sermons have a content of their own and are a separate category from biblical or theological preaching.

On the other hand, the *form* of life-situation preaching commends itself to our attention; that is, if life-situation (or even topical) preaching is considered an *approach* in the sermon rather than the *substance* of the sermon, then life-situation preaching has some reason for existence. For example, in the case cited of a personal problem of suffering, the sermon introduction could well begin with a life-situation example of a couple who have lost a child in a meaningless accident. Such an example could be a "real" life situation out of the parish. The setting up of this problem would certainly be concerned with people, their problems, and the questions they ask. Then, the sermon itself could (need we add, should) be an expository sermon from the Bible, for example, the book of Job, undoubtedly not only discussing Job but the Cross and Resurrection as well. From this base the sermon would grow from biblical insights—the Word of God through the preacher—and be resolved in the light of the gospel proclamation. The sermon could then end (conclusion) with the situation with which the preacher started now enlightened by the gospel message. In this way suffering (Job or many other biblical instances); God working in the affairs of men (Jeremiah); social justice (Amos); race (Christ's death for all men) and other so-called "topics" can be handled within the biblical framework and context. In this way, the sermon remains a sermon —a Christian message to people in need—which is the preacher's only legitimate task in the pulpit. In short, life-situation or topical preaching is highly suspect as a sermon type; as an approach to preaching, it can be highly desirable.

This brings us again to the perspective of this book. What does it mean to proclaim the Word to people? We must once again look at the definition of biblical preaching as proclaiming the gospel (kerygma) through the exposition of specific scriptural material *directed to contemporary life*. The italics are important for our purposes here. *Contemporary life* is where the preacher and his people live. It is where the gospel becomes meaningful to them. The Word is never in a void; it becomes complete when it is responded to in faith. Therefore, the people are not only the recipients of the gospel, but in a sense complete the revelation by responding to it. This was suggested in connection with the concept of the gospel as *incarnational*. The Word *became* flesh; the Word *becomes* flesh in the life of God's people (*laos,* or laity). Although the Word is God's Word, and never man's, God has chosen to reveal himself in Christ, through the Bible, through the preacher, and through the church. In this way, his Word becomes truly revelatory when it is heard and responded to. A solitary voice from a mountaintop results merely in an echo; an answer from another person constitutes a message—a word. Thus, God's Word becomes message when persons hear and respond.

Practically, this means that the preacher is vitally concerned with people. He knows their needs, questions, aspirations, longings, desires, and failures. This is the place where his pulpit and pastoral work intersect. His calling and counseling are indispensable to his preaching. No preacher can know his people sitting in his study. His shepherding—his love—of the flock will acquaint him with his people, enabling him to have tremendous concern that the gospel is made meaningful in their lives. He may be a Christian orator, and neglect his people, but he cannot do so and be a Christian preacher. For the preacher, out of love and understanding, will be eager to relate them to the good news of Christ.

As we have seen, life-situation preaching is a valid way of preaching if it is considered as a concern for people and a desire to keep the gospel relevant on a human level. If it is thought of apart from biblical-theological categories, then it is as incomplete as if the preacher were trying to preach the gospel apart from relevant adaptation to people. It can become humanistic and moralistic if trusted too far away from the biblical context from which the gospel springs. Yet it can be of tremendous value if it reminds the preacher that there are persons in front of him, and that the gospel is meant for those workers, teachers, doctors, and housewives who sit before him week after week.

Person-centered, or topical, preaching does not contradict what we have said about biblical preaching being the norm for our preaching program. It is a false dichotomy to assume that biblical preaching is high and lifted up and that life-situation preaching is relevant. True biblical preaching moves out from its source, and is concerned with meeting the needs of contemporary life—people. Indeed, it is the only valid way of doing so to make sure the gospel is proclaimed and that the Word heard in the final analysis is not a human word but the saving Word.

Actually, the preacher cannot always be sure that he knows his congregation's problems. Indeed, the people themselves may not know their own problems. The difficulties we see are not always the right ones. Surface problems are easily manageable, and cover up the person's real situation. The preacher's own judgment may be faulty in his analysis just as is his congregation's. The Scripture, however, confronts us with real problems rather than the ones we think we see or think we have. A good example of this deeper penetration is the experience of Peter and the lame man. (Acts 3:1-10.) The lame man was seeking alms, but Peter said, "I have no silver and gold, but I give you what I have; in the name of Jesus Christ of Nazareth, walk." Peter saw through what the man asked for to what he really needed. He was asking for alms, but his real problem was the need for wholeness. So it is that the Bible confronts us with our real problems, not with the ones we think we have, which are always chimerical. The one difficulty with Tillich's method of correlation (the culture raises questions; the gospel provides the answers) is that we cannot always know the questions. We may misread them, make wrong judgments on what the real problems of culture are. The Bible, however, speaks to the *real* questions of man. Its dynamic and concrete way of dealing with man's deepest questions is much more effective than dependence upon our own—or others'—ideas of man's needs. One of the greatest contributions of dialectical theology has been at this precise point. It reminds us that the gospel speaks to our needs whether we see them or not—or, indeed, whether we want to see them.

T. S. Eliot reminds us of our own self-deception:

> Why should men love the Church? Why should they love her laws?
> She tells them of Life and Death, and of all that they would forget.
> She is tender where they would be hard, and hard where they like to be soft.
> She tells them of Evil and Sin, and other unpleasant facts.
> They constantly try to escape
> From the darkness outside and within
> By dreaming of systems so perfect that no one will need to be good.
> But the shadow that is will shadow
> The man that pretends to be.[12]

The word "Bible" could easily be substituted for the word "Church" to demonstrate how Scripture speaks to our deepest life situations.

Biblical-doctrinal preaching, then, is not incompatible with a life-situation approach to problems and people. In fact, it is the only valid way to deal with people. Their souls are too precious to be trusted to a human word or to a human's advice. They deserve nothing less than the eternal Word which speaks, judges, forgives, and saves. The preacher would do well to keep his people and their needs always in his mind as he preaches, and at the same

[12] "The Rock." From *The Complete Poems and Plays, 1909-1950* (New York: Harcourt, Brace & World, 1952). Used by permission of Harcourt, Brace & World, and Faber and Faber Ltd.

time concentrate on finding and preaching God's gospel of good news. In short, there is a real sense in which there is only one definition of preaching: an effective sermon is one which is biblically based, doctrinally sound, and has a "life-situation" thrust to it. This is another way of saying that the preacher's task is to proclaim the gospel through the exposition of specific scripture directed to meeting the needs of contemporary life. In this instance, the needs of contemporary life are the souls entrusted to his care.

CHAPTER VI

Proclaiming the Word in Controversy

Controversy is no problem for many preachers. They simply avoid preaching on any theme which might raise a problem or a difference of opinion. These preachers become Reverend Mr. Chameleons, blending in with the cultural mores of the time and their congregations. For them, the Cross has been replaced by the weathervane, and their preaching is determined largely by the way the wind is blowing. They preach to their congregations' delight and dictates. Everything is played safe—the boat is not to be rocked. Their motto might be: "Come weal or come woe my status is quo." Or, to paraphrase Teddy Roosevelt: "Speak softly, and carry a big feather." These are the preachers who are afraid to meet an issue head on or to upset their parishioners. They rather prefer to comfort the afflicted than to afflict the comfortable.

There are other preachers who would avoid controversy on theological grounds. They would say one should never deliberately set out to preach controversy. The preacher's job, they contend, is to preach the great affirmations of the gospel and to avoid topics or current issues which in reality have no place in the pulpit. There is, of course, truth to this allegation, particularly when we consider that topical preaching has gone berserk in many places. Some preachers jump from one headline to another for their source materials like delirious grasshoppers. Many good laymen are tired of hearing about such inconsequential topics as physical fitness from the pulpit.

Nevertheless, "all vital issues are controversial." [1] No preacher can go through life avoiding controversy if his pulpit is to be vital. In the face of the great issues of our time, the preacher cannot stick his head into the sand—ostrich-like—if he is to be relevant. A bombed school, an incident of school integration, a proposal for state support of private schools, an increase in the population's drinking habits, new testing of H-bombs—all or any of these may be the paramount issue any given Sunday morning with the congregation. The preacher who avoids such topics altogether is the model of irrelevancy. If Christ is the Lord of life, then any aspect of our common life can be brought into the light of the Christian gospel, and therefore no vital subject is taboo. It must, however, be pointed out that the method of handling the material may be the key as to whether the material has a worthy place in the Christian pulpit. It is that problem with which we are primarily concerned.

One other thing before considering the way in which controversy is preached. One tends to think of controversy

[1] Quoted in Harold Bosley, *Preaching on Controversial Issues* (New York: Harper & Bros., 1953), p. 15.

in terms of social issues. In the main this may be true, but even a theological issue may be controversial. The preacher who preaches on the miraculous birth of Jesus—regardless of which side he takes—may find himself in a hotbed of controversy.

Also, there seems to be a relationship between geography and controversy. Some preachers can get all upset about drinking, continually preaching abstinence, while they are in the midst of a racial problem and are significantly silent about it. The same with other issues in other areas.

Given the importance and inevitability of preaching on controversies, what is the best way to deal with them? Those who have written on this subject suggest that there are obviously two main ways in which controversy can be handled: one, direct; two, indirect.[2]

Direct. When the word "direct" is used, many things suggest themselves. For one thing, the special days which are set apart in the church year for pulpit emphasis will involve the preacher in speaking directly to a problem. Unless he chooses to ignore the day altogether, sometime during the year he has the opportunity to discuss labor, the United Nations (World Order Sunday), temperance, the Reformation, and race relations. One or two of these might be considered controversial. The use of special days in the church calendar almost makes mandatory the preacher's consideration of the topic announced for the day.

Another meaning of directness is absolute candor. When we say we speak directly to a problem, it means that we do

[2] For example, Bosley, *ibid.,* pp. 21-22.

not beat around the bush but speak to the point, with candor, fearlessly, and without apology. To many preachers, of course, this is the only honorable way to preach—to preach the gospel as they see it and let the chips fall where they may.

There are some honest questions that can be raised both in regard to special days and the "absolute candor" method. In regard to special days, they present some problems in the church's calendar both in terms of substance and strategy.

First, strategy. For one thing, to announce that next Sunday is Commitment Sunday or Race Relations Sunday—with the expected sermon—can readily set up the defenses of the congregation. They may tend to react in one of two ways: either they will be mad and stay home, or they will come out of loyalty and still be mad. Either way they are not going to listen to much or learn anything. Or their attitude can be one of paternalism, which may be worse. In this view, the layman says, "Well, Bob is going to speak about abstaining from alcohol this Sunday. I'll let him have his say. At least I won't hear anything more about it for another year." In this way the preacher is indulged to speak his piece. The laymen are prepared psychologically for the day, and permit their preachers to have their fling. As far as strategy is concerned, the special days present some real problems. They may tend to compartmentalize important issues, whereas they should have recurring emphases throughout the year.

As to the matter of substance, there is another problem. Actually, the special days may interfere with the Christian year. Some denominations schedule a program year with little reference to the Christian year. At the same time many preachers believe that there is a difference between the program year of the church and the Christian year, and that the latter should be given priority. Many times these are sensitive preachers—sensitive on social issues—who feel constrained to follow the Christian year when there is a conflict. When the program year is at variance with the Christian year, these preachers ignore the so-called special days. To give but one example, some Methodist preachers find it difficult to preach on Commitment Sunday in Advent. They may be preaching Advent sermons, and find that liquor is an intrusion on their themes. Often they will take a collection for temperance but ignore it in their sermons. They feel that in this period the gospel proclamation comes first, especially if they feel the rationale for Commitment Day is that the approaching Christmas season will bring an increase in liquor traffic. Thus, special days may tend to isolate important issues for a one-day-a-year emphasis, or they may conflict with the Christian year.

The other meaning of directness has to do with absolute candor. This is to announce some social issue as the topic of the day and plow into it fearlessly and courageously. On the surface, this seems to be the only honest way to deal with it fairly. To pursue this task depends upon high-mindedness, fair-mindedness, and open-mindedness on the part of both the preacher and the congregation. This approach has all the overtones of "Come, let us reason together."

Gene E. Bartlett, recent senior minister of the First Baptist Church in Los Angeles and now president of

Colgate-Rochester Divinity School, is a very able pastor and an outstanding social preacher. He once preached a sermon in the First Baptist Church of Evanston, Illinois, on "What Should Christians Do About Military Training?" He had a very good congregation and they respected him highly. He used this direct approach, stating in the introduction:

> It is only fair to say at the outset that I am opposed to this plan, or any form of permanent military training. Admitting a deep-rooted predisposition against the military approach to both domestic and international problems, I still have tried to listen to the arguments as carefully as possible. But this proposal seems to me to be not only unconvincing in the arguments on its behalf, but dangerous in its implications for our American way of life. Even deeper, it seems to me to threaten many values for which the church stands. Therefore, I frankly speak in opposition to this proposal today and shall mention two broad reasons for this opposition.

This approach recognizes differences, but the preacher honestly presents his ideas, knowing that many of his people may differ, yet he makes his witness and hopes that some will change their minds. He depends on his honesty, his fairness, and his personal integrity as a minister to overcome any hostility. He is also convinced that he is presenting a Christian message, or a message rooted in the Christian gospel.

This seems to be the only honorable way to preach on controversial subjects. People do not like sycophants. Many preachers who skirt around every contemporary social problem receive—secretly at least—contempt from their people. The preacher who is afraid to upset his people or to disagree with them or to take an unpopular stand ends up with their contempt. Conversely, the preacher who preaches his beliefs—though unpopular—if he has respect as a minister of Christ, will win respect from his people, if not agreement.

But in spite of these obvious advantages in speaking directly to a problem, there are also some disadvantages and dangers. It is dangerous to suggest this, for there are so many preachers who do nothing in preaching on controversy. One of the great dangers in preaching candidly on a social problem is illustrated dramatically by so many of our so-called social preachers; that is, they may become self-styled martyrs. Some students leave seminary determined the first Sunday to clear up the people's minds about the virgin birth; the next Sunday, alcohol, and the next, peace. Often these preachers bounce from one church to another all over Christendom, believing themselves to be martyrs for the cause of Christ. They have not been concerned to minister to people and to enlarge their horizons, but have used shock treatment to enhance their own status. Above all, they have failed to recognize that preaching is more than rational assertion or acceptance of an idea. Preaching must reach people emotionally and volitionally to effect change, and the direct approach may not reach these levels. For example, many people will agree with the preacher when he attacks them headlong for drinking, but that of course doesn't motivate them not to drink. Some preachers who speak candidly assume that there is a Christian side to every controversy which is self-evident and which, if spelled out clearly enough and logically enough, will be accepted.

This leads to the second question with the absolute candor method. It often takes the congregation where the preacher wishes them to be rather than where they are. People do not sit in congregations with dispassionate and open minds, waiting to be convinced with logical and rational arguments of the truth of a case. They sit there with prejudices and emotions and fears and frustrations and minds—to be sure—all wrapped up together. The preacher who tries to reach them on only one level—the rational—may not even communicate, let alone motivate. This, of course, gets into the muddy but exciting and necessary waters of persuasion, but it points up the fact that the frontal assault of the absolute candor method may ignore the fact that people are motivated not only by mental argument but by emotional persuasion as well.[3]

The third problem with the absolute candor method is that the preacher does not always get the gospel into the sermon. In an endeavor to meet the social problem with effectiveness, the preacher may spend most of his time sociologically or psychologically, and fail to bring the Christian gospel itself to bear in the sermon. For example, many sermons on race talk about the same blood types, the similar IQ's, environmental factors, etc. These are Red Cross reasons for brotherhood. What does the Christian gospel itself have to say about racial brotherhood? Similarly, many sermons on divorce are based simply on sociological principles. In each of these cases, all the support that can be gathered is necessary, but in the final

[3] For an extended discussion of the relation between persuasion and homiletics, see Ronald E. Sleeth, *Persuasive Preaching* (New York: Harper & Row, 1956).

analysis the people are interested to hear what the gospel itself has to say—if anything—on the subject being discussed.

In spite of these problems, the direct way is a most valid way of preaching to controversy. It has the value of holding up (as in special days) the subject; it gives preparation for the day (expectancy); and it challenges the preacher to meet fearlessly and head on some of the great questions of our time.[4]

Indirect. The other approach to controversy is through the indirect method. It is very dangerous for anyone in these days to suggest an oblique or indirect method of approaching social concerns. It can be open to all sorts of misinterpretation. There are hundreds of ministers who are so oblique or indirect that they never take a stand on anything controversial. Yet, in spite of the inherent dangers, there is a valid indirect way to approach controversial material. In essence, this approach means that the preacher is basically preaching the gospel (or the biblical-theological affirmations of the Christian faith)

[4] The preacher should remember that occasionally he may have to speak boldly, directly, and forthrightly on an issue, regardless of the consequences. He should never encourage such a moment, but he should not flinch if it comes. If people in the church hold to views which are universally accepted as unchristian, and if they persist in such attitudes even after long and patient ministry, then the preacher may have to use the pulpit as a two-edged sword. Although this might be considered the preacher's last resort, he must keep it in mind as a possibility. Shock treatment may be the only "cure" to which a hardened heart may respond. An interesting analysis of this point of view is presented by John H. Marion in an article entitled "Behind Dixie's Gentler Standpatters," *The Christian Century,* October 24, 1962, pp. 1288-90.

Sunday after Sunday and covering social questions in either one of two ways: either through illustrations coming out of a gospel theme which would give a social implication to all his preaching; or, even when confronting some social issue *per se,* to preach it in the context of a so-called gospel message. This, of course, can be an excuse for not preaching fearlessly on any social question. Yet, in spite of this danger, it can be a most effective means of dealing with controversy.

For one thing, this position argues that the main business of the preacher is to preach the gospel, not issues or things. Halford E. Luccock once told a story of a town in the Dakotas that was knocked out during a flash flood. All communication lines were down, and the railroad tracks were washed away. One church, getting nothing from its denominational headquarters about special days for the next two Sundays, decided it was on its own. After much discussion it was suggested that the church worship God.[5] This is a caricature, but it is true that some preachers, after trying desperately to be relevant at all costs, are again discovering that their main task is to preach the riches of God. The average preacher cannot be adequately informed on every cultural or political issue that comes up. He should, however, be an authority in the Christian faith, with its implications and applications both social and personal. This is the gospel of what God has done in Christ, is continuing to do, and the message of reconciliation.

[5] *Like a Mighty Army* (New York: Oxford University Press, 1954), pp. 49-51.

Second, the controversy may be more effectively handled from the point of strategy in the context of theological and biblical material. Although this is a pragmatic consideration, the preacher should not be afraid of that word "strategy," even though when he uses it someone says, "That's manipulation." Nevertheless, if the controversy cannot be handled in the biblical-theological framework, then it is dubious if it is a subject for preaching. If the controversy can be so handled, then it may be the best strategy. Many preachers get shot down by their laymen when they sail out into the wild blue yonder on their own. It is much better to let the laymen take out their wrath on Amos or the gospel.

Third, and like unto the second, it is often more disarming to preach indirectly by basing the material on a biblical-theological framework. Granted that even the gospel itself may be controversial when the people are shaken out of their sinfulness and talked to about the grace of God; nevertheless, the controversial thrust may be more effective if the people are responding to the proclamation of the gospel and then see the concrete implication before their very eyes. This enables them to make the adaptation for themselves from the very impact of the gospel on their lives. Henry Ward Beecher said some sound things on this point that have a contemporary relevance:

When I was settled at Indianapolis, nobody was allowed to say a word on the subject of slavery. They were all red-hot out there then; and one of the Elders said, "If an abolitionist comes here, I will head a mob to put him down." I was a young preacher. I had some pluck; and I felt, and it grew in me, that that was a subject that ought to be preached upon; but I knew that just as sure as I preached an abolition sermon they would blow me up sky high, and my usefulness in that parish would be gone. Yet I was determined they should hear it, first or last. The question was, "How shall I do it?" I recollect one of the earliest efforts I made in that direction was in a sermon on some general topic. It was necessary to illustrate a point, and I did it by picturing a father ransoming his son from captivity among the Algerines, and glorying in his love of liberty and his fight against bondage. They all thought I was going to apply it to slavery, but I did not. I applied it to my subject, and it passed off; and they all drew a long breath.

It was not long before I had another illustration from that quarter. And, so, before I had been there a year, I had gone over all the sore spots of slavery, in illustrating the subjects of Christian experience and doctrine. It broke the ice.

You may say that that was not the most honorable way, and that it was a weakness. It may have been so; but I conquered them by that very weakness.[6]

They began to make their own connections between the gospel and the life they should be living, until in time he was able to deal with the subject more directly.

Finally, as we have seen here previously, preaching from the biblical framework is our normal stance. We are not preaching social issues; we are proclaiming the Word. In this sense, it is not strategy at all; it is our commitment. It so happens that it is an effective way to handle con-

[6]*Yale Lectures on Preaching* (New York: J. B. Ford & Co., 1872), pp. 166-67.

troversy, but we should not forget that we preach biblically in order to proclaim God's Word, not to be strategic.

Thus, there are two valid ways of approaching controversy—indirect and direct. Whichever method is used, there are some principles which should be held up as the basis for controversial preaching. Since some of these have been implied earlier, this will serve as a brief summary.

First of all, whether preaching directly or indirectly to a problem, the preacher should place the material in the context of the gospel. Why else are we preaching? We are primarily ministers and preachers, and our basic task is to preach the gospel of good news. There should be no dichotomy between the ethical implications and the gospel proclamation, but the proclamation ought always to be there.

Second, a good case could be made that the more controversial the sermon, the more expository it should be. This may sound too much like technique, but it is nevertheless good preaching as well as a good approach. A controversial sermon on chauvinism or false national pride might well be handled in the context of Jeremiah, who was one of the first of the great prophets to show that God was in the lives of men and nations and judging them.

Third, the preacher should get all the facts about the subject he is discussing. This is so elementary, and yet many preachers fail here. Preachers are notorious for glaring generalities and unsupported statements. Some preachers' handling of the alcohol problem could easily drive their laymen to drink. Using alcohol and alcoholism synonymously is an example of the kind of spurious reasoning that calls forth smirks and benign smiles from laymen as they listen to their preachers on Commitment Sunday. The preacher's excursion into social areas should be accompanied by a rigorous devotion to truth.

Fourth, the preacher should use the pronouncements of his church. Most of the denominations have forthright statements on social issues. The preacher should stand boldly on these platforms. Granted that the churches are confused and inaudible at times, they do speak out strongly on certain questions. Standing with these statements not only gives the preacher data for his sermon, but also reassures him that he belongs to a wider fellowship which can sustain him in controversy.

Fifth, the preacher should attempt to be positive in his approach. This includes more than just being positive rather than negative; constructive rather than destructive. It also means that the preacher will want to implant a positive program or attitude in place of a faulty, negative, or unchristian attitude or program. He will not want simply to attack race prejudice; he will want to build up positive feelings toward all men by basing his material on the Atonement. He will not only attack alcohol, he will show positive understanding concerning why people drink. He may support the Supreme Court's ruling on state-prescribed prayers, but he will want to show positively how the religious education of our children can be handled in a better way. In short, his task is not to tear down but to build up.

Sixth, the preacher should recognize honest differences. It is sometimes difficult to see the opposite side of some issue about which one feels strongly. Nevertheless, there are often questions upon which sincere Christians differ. Preachers need to recognize the rights of others—Christians and otherwise. Judgmatic attitudes may read fair-minded people out of the church.

Finally, the preacher should speak the truth in love. This is difficult for anyone when he is possessed by righteous indignation. Suffice it to say that some preachers may preach on love with hostility in their faces, eyes, or voice. It is difficult to speak a word of judgment in the context of love, yet it is the best way to win support on the nonrational, volitional level. Some believe that the greatest factor in persuasion—winning the congregation to the response sought—is the character of the preacher. And nowhere would this be more important than in the controversial sermon where the hostility is usually more to the preacher's idea than to the preacher himself.

The method of handling controversy can best be dramatized in a story told about the late, great Ernest Fremont Tittle, who labored valiantly for many years in the First Methodist Church in Evanston, Illinois. Tittle, in a conservative area, preached great social-gospel sermons. What many people forget was that this was a man with a shepherd's heart. One man once related that when his first wife died he was so bitter he would not even talk to Tittle when he came to the house to call. In fact, he stormed out and began to walk in the park by the lake. He noticed that Tittle had followed him and was walking behind him, not saying a word, but just following. After a few hours, Tittle walked up to him and said, "John, I think we had better go home now." Then said the man with tears in his eyes, "After that, Ernest Tittle can say anything to me from the pulpit and I'll take it." Here is the secret to controversial preaching. A preacher who has a grasp of the gospel, a message rooted in biblical truths, a concern for relevancy, and a deep love for people can walk unafraid into any controversy, knowing that his task is to please God, not men.

CHAPTER VII

Proclaiming the Word to Culture: Modern Literature

A local church group once asked a speaker to review a book of his choice before their monthly meeting. After choosing Eliot's *The Cocktail Party* and so notifying the chairman, he was advised in a most courteous way that this book was not suitable because of the adverse reaction which might be caused by the publicity in the papers. In this instance, the speaker capitulated and gave a bland review of an innocuous book which was picked by the group. One could have said that there was probably more gospel in *The Cocktail Party* than had been in that pulpit for years.

Such an incident could well be a parable of our times for the church's relationship to culture in general and, in this particular instance, modern literature. For while we are limiting ourselves here to literature, the discussion could just as well include music, architecture, the plastic arts, etc. The concern is that the church, and specifically the pulpit, take seriously the culture to which the Word is addressed or in which it is proclaimed. (In fact, the pulpit needs to remember that the church and its people are part of that very culture.) We cannot address a letter without knowing the recipient's name. We cannot speak to a culture which we do not know. Thus, the preacher is reminded once again of Tillich's method of correlation. The culture raises the questions; the gospel provides the answers. So the preacher should seek to find the questions which all culture raises; in this particular instance, literature.

We should remind ourselves once again that our working definition of preaching is to proclaim the Word through Scripture to meet the needs of the day (contemporary life). Our concern in this chapter is to know our contemporary scene. Hence, modern literature becomes only one example of the kind of interest a preacher may acquire in understanding his cultural milieu. Although we may be focusing on the advantages of knowing modern literature as a cultural reflector, we should not forget that our main task is preaching. We are to know culture because we are both part of that culture ourselves and because we are called to proclaim God's Word to it. Just as we need to know the question the culture raises, so the culture equally needs to hear the Word proclaimed. For culture is not to be viewed and accepted as it is. The gospel transforms culture.

Indeed, the preacher may not only find questions in culture but some answers as well. It may not only be a case of proclaiming the Word to culture; in a real sense the Word may be found doing its own work in such cultural expressions as literature. It is safe to say that Christian expressions are often found in such natural orders of creation as art and literature and drama. The Word in this sense may be implicative or derivative, but, nevertheless, it is there. Above all, there are the questions—or, to be more specific, the needs and the reflections of modern man to whom the pulpit addresses the Word.

We are, therefore, beginning to see why the preacher must be acquainted with the cultural expressions of which literature is only one example. To be specific, there are at least three reasons why the preacher should be acquainted with such an area as modern literature.

First, the preacher should be interested in modern literature for *aesthetic* reasons. That is, he should be interested in "art for art's sake." He should do so, not because the preacher should be an aesthete or a dilettante, but because he should be concerned for the beautiful as over against concern only for the moral and the useful. Not all the art forms will have the same appeal, but literature, for example (which we also will see is *useful,* if we must use that category), can be enjoyed just for enjoyment's sake. The preacher desperately needs some such expression for what it does to him as a person. Much of the preacher's life is by necessity pragmatic. He is busy getting sermons ready, chairing meetings, calling on the sick. This is not to say that all these duties are either boring or without value. It simply means that the preacher has little leisure time for the development of the man who is first of all a man—even before being a Christian or a preacher. An interest in literature for its own sake will make him a broader man, perhaps even a better man, but in any event a wiser man.

We will leave for a moment the nature of literature and what makes great literature. Granted that much of modern literature is uneven in quality; nevertheless, the preacher who reads widely will become richer as a man, and hence as a preacher. For the broader the preacher is as a man, the better he is as a specific preacher. Like many paradoxes, this one expresses a great truth. The richer his life, the broader and better his tastes, the more sensitivity he has, the better will be his preaching. Of course, it is obvious that literature would help him in relation to source material for his sermons and the ability to speak the language of his audience, but apart from that, there is the general enrichment of his life which makes him a better man. The wider his interests and knowledge, the stronger his *ethos* (his ethical persuasion—that which arises from his character itself). In short, a well-rounded person is a good beginning for the preacher. An aesthetic concern helps make such a well-rounded man.

The *second* reason has already been alluded to. The preacher should be interested in modern literature for *theological* reasons. If preaching is concerned with "meeting the needs of the day" (chapter II), then he should be anxious to delve into a medium in which those needs are graphically mirrored. For, painful as it may be to the preacher, many novelists and playwrights are speaking more realistically about our situation than are many of the theologians and pulpiteers. Or, to put it another way, many of these writers lay bare the nature, fears, dreams, and aspirations of modern man in a more vital way than do the pulpits. Granted it is debatable whether all modern literature gives an accurate view of the nature of man;

it is undoubtedly true that much of this same literature does reveal modern man as he is, or, just as important, as he thinks he is. In either case, the minister should be aware of this image which permeates the culture in which we live. For even after discounting the seamy side of life, which may be plumbed by an author for shock's sake, there is still the great area of literature which reveals that the writer is where people live. He is in touch with people, knows what they think and what motivates them. How many pulpits know modern man that well? They may know the gospel; they may have the Word which is revealed within the Bible, but these avail little if the soil is not known. If revelation is incarnational, then the joining of the Word to the men of our time is indispensable. Thus, knowledge of them and their ways is mandatory.

Many pulpits, however, are busy answering questions no one is asking. They may know the answers, but not the questions. This is as bad as knowing the questions and not the answers. The preacher, then, could well know literature for the insight it gives him into the nature of modern man. He may even be surprised to see the theological categories which are raised in this literature. He may decide that some, if not most, are long on analysis but short on soteriology, but that analysis alone is worth his time. Anyway, soteriology is his job, not the writer's. The preacher may be amazed to discover that the theme of Arthur Miller's *All My Sons* is guilt.[1] He

[1] Robert McAfee Brown has a penetrating analysis of modern literature in an article entitled, "The Christian and Contemporary Literature," *Union Seminary Quarterly Review,* November, 1956. His insights are extremely helpful, and some of my material in this chapter reveals my indebtedness to him.

will perhaps be surprised to find that at least one way of looking at Robert Penn Warren's *All the King's Men* is through the biblical injunction, "The wages of sin is death" (Rom. 6:23). The modern writer may be dealing with themes which are after all familiar to the preacher, even though the guise may be different.

And he will unfortunately find that in many instances the drama or playwright will be speaking to and about modern man in a way in which he cannot; that is, the medium itself is more pictorial, in the case of a play, or even a novel, which deals more with narration and description, than the average pulpit seems able to do. In so doing, the artist portrays the scene without having to talk *about* it. He *dramatizes* the idea, and the listener or reader participates in it himself through empathy and sympathetic attraction. This is not to say that the pulpit cannot do it, but it often does not, and the artist's medium has this advantage built in. This is what we are concerned to call *existential.* The drama speaks to us at all levels of our existence; we see ourselves there. Our emotions, wills, depths, minds, total being are immersed in the picture before us. The Greeks had the same idea in relation to catharsis and drama. Many of the Greek dramas portrayed on stage the battles and struggles of forces which beset man; the audience, by participating through sympathetic attraction, left the arena purged emotionally, a healthy release for their own lives. Anyone who has witnessed a Judith Anderson in *Medea* has known this same feeling in the modern era. We can have this identification with the characters when we see others involved. We can verily see our own lives on the stage or on the page.

The language of the playwright or the novelist is designed for this kind of response. In a real sense it has similarities with Kierkegaard's concept of indirect discourse. The audience is talked to or "gotten through to" indirectly. Directly, they are being confronted by a pictorial slice of life. Indirectly, they are being confronted on the deepest levels of their own existence. It is more than just representational writing; it is impressionistic and realistic all at the same time. The modern writer lays bare his characters; he has depth and in his writing reveals the nature of man. How many of us have felt this as we watched Willy Loman in Arthur Miller's *Death of a Salesman*. Not only do we see modern man in Willy Loman, but we see the Willy Loman in ourselves. We might wish that there were a different third act, or that Miller were a Christian, or that T. S. Eliot could have written Act III. But all this is speculation, and asks of the playwright something he doesn't want to do or be. The point is, Miller gives us a picture of modern man in a striking way seldom found in a pulpit. We should not ask Miller to preach for us—we can do that—but we must listen and watch, for there are Lomans in our pews, and indeed in our pulpits.

Many preachers are bothered by modern writers because their writings seem so "naturalistic" or "dirty" or "filthy." It is possibly true that some writers deliberately try to shock their readers or sell books by indulging in pornographic writing. But the preacher's moralistic bent must not permit him to make too many generalizations about modern literature. For we often judge writers as if they should be preachers—or at the very least moralists.

We don't want to take them as we find them. The writers are not preachers; they are men writing about life as they see it. In so writing, they do not dodge their responsibilities by covering up the seamy side of man's nature. As writers, they report man at his worst as well as his best. They see his innermost thoughts, desires, lusts, and aspirations as well as the surface veneer that he shows to the world. In so doing, the writer is living up to his responsibility as a writer. Actually, the Bible never slides over the unpleasant in man. It never ducks its responsibility to show the unpleasant as well as the pleasant. There is a lot of "naturalism" in the Bible, but this does not make it filthy; it makes it true. The biblical writers never desired to show only the good side of man. In this sense it is one of the most realistic books ever written. The great David, servant of God, was also the David who coveted Bathsheba.

Many times we may shun modern literature and urge our people to read "religious novels." Undoubtedly there are a few such which deserve to be considered, but much of the so-called religious literature is neither good religion nor good literature. Many reflect an outdated or incorrect view of man; many of them are poorly written. The Christian minister may do well to delve into good literature which is not explicitly Christian or religious; he will be surprised how often he finds material which is implicitly Christian or, better still, material which reflects life as it is. He can then reflect on it or use it or discard it as a Christian minister. The main thing is that he should not ask the writer to be a preacher; that is the minister's job.

He should also remember that many of the writers,

although seemingly revelling in evil by portraying it so graphically, are in a sense moralists themselves, although not explicitly so. The evil in a novel or a play is often judged by the writer. Robert Penn Warren writes sympathetically of Willie Stark in *All the King's Men,* yet it is clear all through the novel that Willie will have a judgment day—and he does. Above all, even though the writer does not always condemn and judge the way we should like, he does manage to maintain a love for creature man. This is something any preacher could emulate in his dealings with people. Alan Paton has a wonderful line which shows his compassion for a character who breached the moral code. He says, speaking of our tendency to judge the wrongdoer, "For God is both Lover and Judge of men, and it is His commandment that we join Him in loving, but to judge we are forbidden." [2]

The *third* reason the preacher should be concerned with modern literature is unashamedly a *pragmatic* one. The materials he reads, for the reasons given, will help him in his understanding of the culture to which he addresses himself; and it therefore follows that much of the material he reads will get into his sermons as illustrations, as background, or as a springboard for his sermons. True, he should not go at his reading as a homiletic Shylock, seeking to carve his pound of flesh from all that he reads. Nevertheless, such saturation with literature will permit him to draw widely from his reading for his sermonic materials. His reading should not be strictly instrumental; but since reading is a creative experience, it will affect

[2] *Too Late the Phalarope* (New York: Signet Books, 1956), p. 176.

him as he prepares his sermons. Illustrations will flash into his mind; insights will come to him through pages of literature. This does not mean his biblical reading is to be neglected. What we are saying does not contradict what we said about biblical preaching. Literary material can be used in an expository sermon, for that matter. The point is that contemporary literature will not only provide the preacher with an understanding of modern man, but also provide materials and pictures of him which are usable in his preaching.

The literature will not always have to be used negatively either; that is, the materials are not necessarily horrible examples. Indeed, in the Tillichian sense, he may find much of it is religious literature in its own right. Or at least he will if he defines "religious" as asking the ultimate questions of life and death: Why are we here? Where are we going? These questions permeate much modern literature, and in that sense are a fertile field for the preacher to plow. We have already alluded to the fact that much so-called Christian literature may not be either Christian or literature. The preacher may thus find himself using "religious" literature which is not labeled as such.

Besides these three reasons for the preacher's being concerned with literature, there is another major consideration which should not escape our attention. There seems to be a correlation between trends in literature and that of religion or theology. One could draw, in many instances, parallel lines—one showing literature and one theology—and the undulations of both would be similar. Interestingly enough, this is often so with the fields oblivious to each other. There is no special correlation between the one and the other, at least not necessarily so. Other factors may, of course, be involved. It could be argued that both of these are affected by outside forces, such as culture itself; that is, changes in culture cause derivative effects of which religion and literature are two examples. Hence, the similarities. Nevertheless, it is clear for our purposes to demonstrate that there is such a relationship. Occasionally they overlap, as when a distinctive Christian writer concerns himself with theology, or when the church enters the field of art, but the correlation may be there even though there is no conscious bridging.

The separation of the two, historically speaking, is a recent innovation. At one time the "arts" and religion were one. In the Middle Ages, the church and the artists were blended. Art was based upon theological suppositions. Not that that period was necessarily a golden age, but it simply means that art and literature were at one time respectable enough to belong within the church. Actually, the Reformation itself had a great deal to do with the divorce. With the Reformation—and especially through the growth of Puritanism, with its iconoclasm and its emphasis upon the plain and unostentatious in religion—came a schism between religion and the arts. The latter were separated from the church. As we know, the breach is still there, although there have been mighty endeavors to heal it. Nevertheless, they do affect each other as the tides of the sea respond to the moon, even though they are not integrally joined. They seem to parallel and reflect the same thought patterns, even if they are on separate tracks.

We can see this illustrated if we look at it historically.

For example, in the period of Rationalism in our own country the dominant religious motif was Deism. God was impersonal and removed; man was dignified and rational. The belletristic literature was largely embellishment. Poetry, for example, which was emotionally oriented could not be a means of truth. The best-known American writers of the age, therefore, were informational and utilitarian. They were the political writers who wrote from the deistic stance—Paine, Jefferson, and Franklin.

The Romantic period which followed was the opposite in some respects. Whereas there was still the goodness and dignity of man, they were coupled with a sentimentalization of religion, an emphasis upon intuition, a rejection of man's fall, and a great emphasis upon pantheism. In the realm of literature, there was a greater corresponding change. In the romantic age, metaphysics evolved out of poetry rather than vice versa. We had the "renascence of wonder" and the return to nature in poetry. Poetic truth became a way of knowledge. The writers of the time illustrate the point admirably: Wordsworth, Emerson, Whitman, and to a lesser extent, Browning.[3]

Now, of course, such generalizations are never absolute, and categorizing tends to oversimplify. In the period we are just describing, there were exceptions to the rule. Randall Stewart uses the category "counter-romantics," to illustrate the fact that such men as Hawthorne and Melville (Henry James at a later period) never succumbed

[3] Randall Stewart has a longer and more thorough discussion of this historical development of American literature. His insights have been of inestimable value to me in this particular section. Cf.: Randall Stewart, *American Literature and Christian Doctrine* (Baton Rouge: Louisiana State University Press, 1958).

to the romantic movement. To this American list could be added such men as Poe and Twain. Dostoevski, who wrote at the same time, also pictured man as a more complex entity than did the romantics. These counter-romantics pictured man as heroic—his heights and depths; his struggles. There is no heroic character when the man is all good or all evil. The romantics tended toward the former; the naturalists at a later day tended toward the latter. The counter-romantics tried to keep their characters in tension between their goodness and badness; hence, they were more heroic in the true sense. But the counter-romantics were not dominant in the nineteenth century. The romantics were; and corresponding to this romanticism in literature was the growth of liberalism in religion, with its increasing emphasis upon the goodness of man.[4]

The twentieth century has brought a change in regard to both religion and literature. We are probably familiar with the changes in religion, but it is well to keep in mind that there have been similar changes in literature. These changes are much too complex to make easy classifications, but some motifs are clear enough. The revolt in literature against romanticism resulted in a kind of naturalism or realism. The revolt in theology against an earlier kind of liberalism is clear to any student of religion. What is of

[4] Stewart defines orthodoxy (both in religion and literature) as whether or not the author subscribes to the doctrine of original sin. "I have insisted upon certain tests of Christian orthodoxy—the chief test being a recognition of Original Sin—and I have tried to make it clear that while certain great writers meet these tests sufficiently to be called 'orthodox,' others—and among them, some of our most famous, influential, and 'democratic' writers—have unmistakably strayed beyond the bounds of Christian orthodoxy." *Ibid.*, pp. viii-ix. This insight, while provocative, does not directly concern us here.

importance here is to see that there is a relationship between the two areas. Corresponding to the naturalism based upon scientific determinism, which is reflected in the novels of Zola, Dreiser, and James T. O'Farrell, on the side of "religion" we see in extreme form a kind of nihilism (or no faith) and existentialism represented by the works of Sartre and Kafka. A good example of the amoralism of the naturalists is the important novel *An American Tragedy* by Theodore Dreiser. In this book the "hero" is doomed almost from the beginning. His doom is sealed through factors of heredity and environment over which he has very little control. The atheistic existentialism of Sartre and Kafka can be seen in almost any one of their works.

Later literature moved into a neorealism or neonaturalism, and theology into what has been called neo-orthodoxy. The neonaturalists in literature saw the sinfulness of man (as over against the liberals of another period), but they also saw his possibilities. In this way, the characters are heroic in that they struggle between the good and evil within them. This makes for heroes. Men like William Faulkner, Robert Penn Warren, and Arthur Miller are examples of this particular strain of literary effort. On the theological side, the religious world has been greatly affected by the writings of Karl Barth, the Niebuhrs, and Paul Tillich. These men too, revolting from an earlier liberalism in religion, emphasized once again the biblical views of man, including his sinfulness, all the while trying to hold on to the truths gained through the liberal revolt against fundamentalism. We need not recount here the influence of this important movement in the religion of our time.

These religious and literary motifs have overlapped at many points; consciously, in such men as T. S. Eliot and W. H. Auden, who are products of their literary age and at the same time are writing consciously as Christians. In such writers we see a blend between the theological stirrings of the time and the dominant literary motifs. Although not as consciously Christian, the same thing can be seen to a lesser extent in William Faulkner, and perhaps even Camus, as demonstrated in his book *The Fall.* Unconsciously, these dual concerns appear in many of the modern writers, including such ones as Nathaniel West and J. D. Salinger, to name only two.

What are these ideas which seem to permeate both traditions? At the risk of oversimplification it can be said with some assurance that such things as the conflict between good and evil; man at war with himself (*Angst*); the use of existential categories, including the probing of the psychological depths of man; the dynamic relationship of human beings; and the use of symbol and myth as conveyors of truth are the dominant themes which are the concerns of both religion and literature of the present day. Nathan Scott [5] has pointed out that modern literature is

[5] No one has been more articulate about the relationships between theology and literature than has Nathan Scott. All of us who are interested in these areas are indebted to him. For those who wish to do additional reading, the following three books are recommended highly: Nathan A. Scott, Jr., *Modern Literature and the Religious Frontier* (New York: Harper & Row, 1958); Nathan A. Scott, Jr., *Rehearsals of Discomposure* (New York: Columbia University Press, 1952); Nathan A. Scott, Jr. (ed.), *The Tragic Vision and the Christian Faith* (New York: Association Press, 1957).

concerned with imagination, and modern religion with the will. If so, we can see how these two streams converge at the point of the nonlogical, nonrational level of human endeavor.

There are indications that both fields are developing in new directions. This is as it should be; for neither field is static, but constantly changing. The interesting thing is that this development again seems to go hand in hand. On the side of religion, we are told that we are in a post–neo-orthodox period. Some refer to it as neo-liberalism. The new quest for the historical Jesus, the interest in comparative religion, and a new concern for philosophical matters are all indications that theology is moving onto a new or different frontier. There are similar indications that literature is moving to a newer posture, perhaps more life affirming. Whatever the future holds—and no one can be sure where we are going in either field—it is fruitful to see how religion and culture (in this instance manifested in literature) go hand in hand.

Kierkegaard has suggested that the three stages of man's quest are aesthetic, moral, and religious. It is interesting to note that, while the first two are not fulfilling in themselves, they do have meaning after the third stage has been reached and one looks back and indeed redeems his former state. This has relevance here; for as one grows in religious awareness, changes his position, and develops new insights, he may find that what was once an inadequate expression of his faith can be revisited with new eyes. For example, Robert Browning was cast aside by many people as a hopeless romantic when their theological insights went beyond an optimistic liberalism. He may have been quoted in derision for saying, "God's in his heaven. All's right with the world," and "Grow old along with me! the best is yet to be." Yet, after maturing in newer theological insight and perhaps retreating a bit from the extreme of reaction, they can now read Browning and find in him more than naïve optimism. Such a realization demonstrates the futility of rigid categories and shows that the great changes are perhaps in ourselves.

Although we have spent considerably more time on literature than on preaching *per se* in this final chapter, the reasons are critically important. The preacher lives in a world of culture which he ignores at his own peril. He can become the model of irrelevancy by ignoring such fields as modern literature. This material will be familiar to his people. The concerns of his congregation may be mirrored for him in such writings. To know their questions, he must be alert to those who reflect our times. But more than this neutral concern, he will find gropings—and indeed affirmations—being made which in themselves may be the vehicles for transmitting the gospel. Above all, he will be conscious of the desperate need to proclaim the Word to this broken world. For what has been said does not deny the kerygmatic nature of his preaching or the biblical roots of the gospel. Indeed, those are the wellsprings of his life. He can only speak a word when he has listened to the Word. As he stands in two worlds he will be trying frantically to join the two, as he sees the crying need to relate man's need to God's grace.

But it is also true that the gospel becomes gospel only when it is heard and received. That is why the emphasis here on our culture. We need to know our culture, realize we are a part of it, and use its language and forms to enrich our lives, our pulpits, and make effective our evangelism. Our preaching is to proclaim the Word through Scripture, to be sure, but it is also directed to meeting the needs of contemporary life. The glory of the Christian faith is that the Word continues to become flesh to those who hear the Word, but only if the Word is made meaningful to modern man where he is and in the categories he understands.

INDEX